Women ADHD Falling through the Cracks

Unmasking the Bias and Exploring Why ADD and ADHD Symptoms in Adult Women and Girls Are Misunderstood and Undiagnosed

Rachel Wright

Thank You!

Thank you for your purchase.

I am dedicated to making the most enriching and informational content. I hope it meets your expectations and you gain a lot from it.

INTRODUCTION

The majority of research on attention deficit hyperactivity disorder (ADHD) has traditionally focused on males, who were believed to make up 80% of all those with ADHD. Now more and more females are being identified, especially now that we are more aware of the non-hyperactive subtype of ADHD. Girls and women with ADHD struggle with a variety of issues that are different from those faced by males. This book will highlight some of those differences, and we will explore the types of struggles faced by females with ADHD.

ADHD is a neurodevelopmental disorder characterized by impulsive behavior and related symptoms. The disorder is classified into three types: impulsive/hyperactivity, inattention/distractibility, and a combination.

While ADHD is the most common disorder among boys aged four to eleven, only about half as many girls are diagnosed, according to the Australian Institute of Health and Welfare. While women tend to develop ADHD later in life, most symptoms appear in infancy and go undiagnosed, untreated, or are well-masked by social and communication abilities.

According to Mark Bellgrove, a professor of cognitive

neuroscience, females with ADHD are more likely than males to abuse substances. He stated, "As a result, we want to catch them sooner and treat them more effectively. However, I believe it is safe to say they are slipping through the cracks."

According to some studies, up to three-quarters of adult women with ADHD are undiagnosed. Many women diagnosed with ADHD as adults reflect on the red flags they ignored as children, such as difficulties in school or difficulties making friends. They wonder how their lives would have changed if their condition had been identified earlier. Coping with symptoms becomes more difficult for those not diagnosed as their responsibilities grow in adulthood.

According to ADHD-specialist psychologist Tamara May, some women receive an ADHD diagnosis after years of struggling with symptoms of "secondary" depression and anxiety due to the problem not being diagnosed. "During adolescence, many women realize they are struggling more than their classmates, but they don't know why," she adds. People underestimate the severity of ADHD and how difficult even the most basic tasks can be. "You're being lazy; you should be able to do better," people around them say. Simply getting up and doing the dishes can be a challenge.

This medical issue is exacerbated by the fact that there are a limited number of psychiatrists who specialize in ADHD, almost all of whom work in the private sector. According to Dr. May, it is extremely rare for someone to be diagnosed in the public hospital system. "Women must first recognize that they are experiencing symptoms of ADHD before consulting with their primary care physician and obtaining a referral to see a private psychiatrist. Waitlists range from three to six months, and some psychiatrists have closed their doors." Some women have reported spending up to $2,000 to get a diagnosis confirmed.

Furthermore, obtaining ADHD medication necessitates a consultation with a psychiatrist. Women who want to change their lives by recognizing and accepting their ADHD must take the initiative. While public awareness of adult ADHD is growing, research biases persist. Women's specific complications such as the effects of pregnancy, menopause, hormones, and the menstrual cycle on ADHD symptoms have received little attention.

Women are just as negatively affected by ADHD as men, if not more so. While most ADHD research has focused on white male participants, some studies have included or focused on the life outcomes of adult female ADHD patients. This book does a detailed analysis and provides helpful solutions.

ADHD is a disorder with a high comorbidity rate. It has been determined that ADHD in a girl or woman increases the likelihood that she will experience trauma at some point in her life. The most common comorbid diagnoses in women are depression, anxiety, and eating disorders. While these diagnoses frequently co-occur, it has been discovered that many women are misdiagnosed with conditions such as anxiety or depression when the underlying issue is ADHD. Unintended pregnancies, marital abuse, and an increased risk of self-harm and suicide are more common in women with ADHD than in the general population. While the literature indicates that living with ADHD hurts both men and women, gender differences among people with ADHD have not been thoroughly investigated. However, this research is necessary because the number of women diagnosed with ADHD has risen in recent years. This is partly due to practitioners' increased awareness that not only can ADHD persist into adulthood, but it is also not a gender-based illness.

Women whose disabilities or struggles may have gone unnoticed or been misinterpreted during childhood and adolescence struggle to cope with the inevitable increase in adult responsibilities. This trend has been picked up and written about in the popular press. Many doctors and psychiatrists agree that a lack of research is a problem. They believe that advances in this area could reduce stigma and provide greater inclusion for people with ADHD and other illnesses.

Despite the bad press and lack of research, there are success stories. Ms. Josie Bober's is one. Despite consistently high grades, Ms. Bober had been unable to complete any of the university degrees she had begun before her diagnosis. Despite her illness, she recently completed a graphic design degree and is now determined to help others by making universities more welcoming to neurodiverse people. Her alma mater, the University of New South Wales, has even provided her with funding to conduct workshops with students and professors to develop effective strategies. In her interview, she stated, "I was feeling proactive. I believe I reached a point within myself where I felt confident and eager to help others. "Increased ADHD diagnoses among women should improve their overall performance and quality of life. However, a lack of research on women with ADHD may result in gender-specific requirements and overlooked obstacles in this population."

This book offers a comprehensive insight into the identification, treatment, and support for girls and women with ADHD. It is critical to reject the widely held belief that ADHD is a behavioral disorder and concentrate on the more subtle and internalized presentation typical of females. Adopting a lifelong model of care is critical to assist the multiple transitions that females experience concurrently with changes in their clinical presentation and social situations. Treatment with pharmacological and psychological therapies is expected to increase productivity, reduce resource use, and, most importantly, better the long-term outcomes for girls and women. This book is a must-have for any girl or woman who thinks she may have ADHD!

CHAPTER 1: UNDERSTANDING ADHD

Attention Deficit Hyperactivity Disorder (ADHD) is a neurological condition that affects a person's thoughts, behaviors, and ability to process information. It mainly affects children and adolescents; however, it may affect adults too. Approximately 11 percent of children between four and seventeen have ADHD, and around four percent of adults in the U.S. suffer from the condition. It's three times more common in boys than girls.

19

ADHD is classified as a neurodevelopmental disorder, similar to disorders such as autism, and is not a mental illness. Neurodevelopmental conditions arise when the nervous system's development is compromised during the early stages of childhood. This is due to a combination of genetic, neurological, and environmental factors.

ADHD comes in three types: Inattentive, Hyperactive-Impulsive, and Combination. Each type of ADHD is associated with one or more distinguishing features. Individuals with the inattentive form are easily distracted and have difficulty concentrating and organizing their thoughts. Individuals with the hyperactive-impulsive type often fidget when speaking and struggle to stay focused on a job. Finally, those with the combination type of ADHD often interrupt while others are talking, appear not to listen when spoken to, become easily distracted, and are fond of taking risks.

You can only know the type of ADHD you have based on your symptoms. Because everyone is unique, two individuals may have the same symptoms yet interpret them differently. Males and females, for example, often behave differently anyway. Males could be seen as more energetic, whereas girls may be viewed as calmer and more uninterested in risky behavior.

Recent Studies and Statistics

Until recently, ADHD was thought to be a disorder that only affected children. According to the most recent estimates, 9.6 percent of children between the ages of three and 17 have been diagnosed with this issue. According to novel research published in the *American Journal of Psychiatry*, about 10 percent of persons with ADHD grow out of it. Even if individuals have symptom-free periods, 90 percent will suffer from at least moderate symptoms throughout adulthood. This study's authors considered ADHD an episodic condition with symptoms that vary and change based on life circumstances. Many children with ADHD, for example, may seem to be symptom-free at the age of 18 while still in high school and living at home. When those same teenagers go off to college, their ADHD symptoms may resurface owing to the stress that often comes with a change in environment. Experts have long known that anxiety and lack of sleep may exacerbate ADHD symptoms. These researchers intend to focus their future study on potential causes and supports for patients with ADHD. The results collated from the Multimodal Treatment of Attention Deficit Hyperactivity Study (MTA), a federally sponsored experiment, are presented in this report.

The MTA began in 1998 and followed roughly 600 children from the ages of seven to nine until they reached the age of 25. They lived at eight different locations throughout the nation.

The Centers for Disease Control and Prevention (CDC) conducted a study in 2016. They discovered that around 6.1 million children between the ages of two and 17 (9.4 percent) had been diagnosed with ADHD. The condition has also been identified in 388,000 (2.4 percent) children aged two to five, 2.4 million (9.6 percent) school-aged children aged six to 11 years, and 3.3 million (13.6 percent) teenagers aged 12 to 17 years. Based on their research, the CDC concluded that males are more likely than females to be diagnosed with ADHD. (12.9 percent and 5.6 percent, respectively).

However, new research shows that ADHD affects a more significant percentage of females than is often recognized. Because of how girls' symptoms develop compared to boys', ADHD may be overlooked in females, indicating a general bias in the diagnosing process. According to the DSM-5, ADHD is one of childhood's most frequent neurodevelopmental disorders. While estimates vary, the global incidence of ADHD in adolescents is about 5 percent.

According to a study by the Centers for Disease Control and Prevention (CDC) in 2016, the global prevalence of adult ADHD is predicted to be 2.8 percent. Adult ADHD prevalence estimates in the United States vary. According to one research paper published in 2019, the prevalence of adult ADHD is 0.96 percent, up from 0.43 percent a decade before. Adult ADHD prevalence rates in the United States have previously been estimated to range between 2.5 percent and 4.4 percent, with males being diagnosed at 5.4 percent compared to 3.2 percent for women.

ADHD Brain VS Normal Brain

Researchers discovered that the cerebral cortex, limbic system, and reticulating activating systems in individuals with ADHD are distinct from those of others. These differences explain short attention spans, learning problems, emotional instability, and restlessness. The cerebral cortex is the brain's outermost layer and is responsible for our highest mental abilities like thought, reasoning, and language. It has been shown that patients with ADHD exhibit slower brain wave activity. Through brain imaging studies, researchers were able to identify that the right frontal lobe of those with ADHD is also smaller than the frontal lobe in individuals without ADHD. This part of the brain is responsible for paying attention, focusing, and concentrating. It is in charge of planning, making choices, learning, remembering, and acceptable behavior. The cortex controls impulse and improper behavior by "inhibitory mechanisms" in the cortex.

The limbic system is the region of the brain located just above the brain stem. It is responsible for one's feelings, motivations, and survival instinct. The limbic system also regulates what is recalled and where memories are kept in the brain. The limbic system – consisting of the hypothalamus, amygdala, and hippocampus – helps us respond to emotional stimuli and is responsible for integrating our bodily senses to make sense of what is happening in the world around us, such as temperature changes, body position, and hormone levels. If the limbic system gets overwhelmed or receives excessive information from the body simultaneously, problems can occur.

The reticulating activating system (RAS) is also found near the spinal cord at the base of the brain. It receives information about the world and one's own body through the senses. It activates cerebral cortex neurons which are in charge of circadian rhythms (sleep and wake cycles), central nervous system activity, and attention. When the RAS is underactive, it causes learning, memory, and self-control problems. However, when the RAS is overactive, the individual becomes easily startled, speaks excessively, and becomes anxious and hyperactive. A shutdown of the RAS causes the loss of consciousness or coma.

Neurodiversity

There's a lot of debate over whether ADHD should be classified as a mental illness. Even though some persons with ADHD exhibit mental abnormalities and severe impairment, some experts still do not consider these abnormalities to indicate a disorder. Instead, they consider these anomalies as usual but extreme.

The term "neurodiversity" is used by researchers to characterize normal, hereditary, brain-based behavioral variances. Certain conditions, classified as diseases, show a total and utter departure from normal and healthy functioning (e.g., diabetes). Similarly, certain conditions are not disease states, yet not everyone has them. For instance, pregnancy. In both circumstances, though, it's all or nothing. You can't be a little bit pregnant or diabetic. These conditions either affect you or do not affect you. Consider it as if you were switching on a light. It can only be turned on or off.

However, unlike many biologically-based symptoms, behavioral symptoms may be a question of degree. There are certain behaviors that almost everyone exhibits to some extent (e.g., inattention). Consider it like a dimmer switch with an endless intensity range between on and off. ADHD is similar to a light switch with a light. It's defined by a set of characteristics (inattention, impulsivity, excessive energy, and distraction) that everyone exhibits to varying degrees. As a result, the issue becomes: At what point does it constitute a disorder?

According to the neurodiversity argument, ADHD is not an unnatural condition since a considerable section of the population exhibits ADHD-like behaviors, although to a lesser degree. It's just an extreme case of a standard variety. As previously stated, to add to the confusion, symptoms such as impulsivity and high energy are not exclusive to ADHD. These signs and symptoms may be seen in a variety of illnesses. The fact that ADHD symptoms aren't exclusive to that condition supports the neurodiversity argument that ADHD isn't an actual disorder.

What Are the Symptoms of ADHD?

Adults with ADHD may have difficulty listening carefully, impulsivity, and anxiety. The signs and symptoms might be modest to severe. While some individuals with ADHD have fewer symptoms as they get older, others have significant symptoms that affect their daily routine.

Many adults with ADHD aren't even aware that they have it; all they know is that regular activities are challenging for them. Adults with ADHD may have trouble focusing and prioritizing, leading to missed deadlines and forgotten meetings or social activities. The inability to manage impulses may manifest in various ways, from irritation when standing in a queue or driving in traffic to bouts of depression and angry outbursts.

Impulsivity, difficulty with multitasking, poor planning, poor organizational skills, disorientation, and issues with prioritizing are some of the symptoms of adult ADHD—as well as low tolerance for frustration, regular mood fluctuations, and issues with completing tasks.

Inattentive ADHD

Inattentive ADHD (often called ADD) manifests as forgetfulness, disengagement, or distractibility, and can be mistaken for anxiety or a mood disorder in adults. Those with inattentive ADHD make mistakes because they cannot stay focused, organize tasks or activities, or follow instructions. They often lose things and become easily distracted by certain external stimuli. Here are some symptoms of Inattentive-Type ADHD:

- Often fails to give close attention to details or makes careless mistakes
- Easily distracted
- Often does not seem to listen when spoken to directly
- Often has trouble organizing tasks and activities

- Often avoids, dislikes, or is reluctant to do tasks that require mental effort over a long period

- Often loses things necessary for tasks and activities

- Forgetful

- Ignores tasks they find boring

- Difficulty learning new information

- Frequent "spaciness"

- Daydreams regularly

Co-occurring Conditions with ADHD

Learning disabilities -- Learning disabilities make it difficult for a child to master certain skills, such as reading or arithmetic. While ADHD is not a learning disability, it can make it difficult for a child to do well in school. Diagnosing learning disabilities requires assessments such as IQ and academic achievement

33

tests. Such disabilities require educational interventions once identified.

Oppositional defiant disorder or conduct disorder – Up to 35 percent of children with ADHD also have an oppositional defiant disorder or conduct disorder. Children with such disorders tend to lose their cool quickly. In addition, they are defiant and hostile towards authority figures. Children with conduct disorder break rules, destroy things, and often get suspended or expelled from school. Children with co-occurring conduct disorder are at much higher risk of having problems with the law or substance abuse than children with ADHD alone. Studies show that this co-existing condition is more common among children with the mainly hyperactive/impulsive type of ADHD and the combined type of ADHD.

Mood disorders/depression – Approximately 18

percent of children with ADHD also have mood disorders such as depression or bipolar disorder (previously called manic depression). There is often a family history of these types of disorders. Co-existing mood disorders can put children at higher risk for suicide, especially during the teen years. These disorders are more common among children who have the inattentive type of ADHD and the combined type of ADHD.

Anxiety disorders – Anxiety affects about 25 percent of children with ADHD. Children with anxiety disorders have extreme feelings of fear, worry, or panic that make it difficult to function. These disorders can produce physical symptoms such as rapid heartbeat, sweating, diarrhea, and nausea. Different counseling and medications may be needed to treat these co-existing conditions.

Language disorders – Children with ADHD may have difficulty with the way they use language. This is known as a *pragmatic language disorder*. It may not show up on standard language tests. A speech and language specialist can detect this by observing how the child uses language in their daily activities.

Diagnosing ADHD

A physical examination, such as a blood test or an X-ray, cannot diagnose ADHD. An assessment technique is used instead by a health professional to diagnose ADHD. Regardless of how ADHD manifests—inattentive, hyperactive-impulsive, or combined—several characteristics must be satisfied before an official diagnosis can be made.

Some of these requirements include:

1. Presence of symptoms before the age of twelve.

2. Observed symptoms should be evident in a variety of circumstances.

3. Observed symptoms have to interfere with or affect one's daily routine.

4. No other mental health disease can explain the symptoms.

A medical interview with a mental health expert qualified to assess and diagnose Attention Deficit Hyperactivity Disorder (ADHD) is used to diagnose the disorder in children and adolescents. Mental health professionals, psychologists, and neurologists that focus on dealing with children and adolescents are the most prevalent practitioners in this field. Neuropsychological testing may help reach a diagnosis, but it is insufficient without a clinical evaluation. Brain imaging techniques such as MRI, CT, and PET scans are not used to diagnose ADHD in children because none of these tools can be used as accurate tools to identify the condition. They may help give the diagnosing professional extra information, but they are not diagnostic on their own.

A child must show at least six ADHD symptoms of inattention, hyperactivity-impulsivity, or both to be diagnosed with ADHD. To establish that a child has ADHD, the symptoms must have been present for at least six months and must have appeared before age seven.

The most common symptoms observed include having trouble keeping attention, listening or following directions, making careless errors, avoiding jobs that demand continuous concentration, being forgetful, becoming sidetracked quickly, and losing things easily.

ADHD in Children

Children with ADHD may have poor self-esteem, strained relationships, and poor academic achievement. Symptoms may reduce as they become older. Some individuals, however, never fully recover from their ADHD symptoms. They can, however, develop effective coping tactics.

Medications and behavioral approaches are often used together in treatment. While medication will not cure ADHD, it may significantly reduce its symptoms. Early detection and treatment may have a significant impact on the person's quality of life.

Inattention and hyperactive-impulsive behavior are two of the most common symptoms of ADHD. ADHD symptoms appear before the age of 12 and in some children start at the age of three. ADHD symptoms

39

may vary from mild to severe and can last well into adulthood.

Males are more likely than females to have ADHD, and behaviors between males and females might vary. Males, for example, may be more hyperactive, while females may be more inattentive.

A child with a pattern of inattention may frequently find it difficult to pay close attention to details or make silly mistakes in coursework, have a hard time staying engaged with activities or play, appear not to pay any attention even when spoken to directly, have trouble following through on directions, and inability to complete school assignments or household duties.

ADHD can be exceedingly devastating, and children diagnosed with the disorder have a greater chance of developing cognitive, behavioral, and psychological issues throughout their childhood than children who do not have the disorder.

It's not surprising that many children with ADHD have issues with social interaction. The primary symptoms of ADHD may have a significant effect on relationships with family members, friends, and guardians. In addition to the primary symptoms of inattention, hyperactivity, and impulsivity, challenges with interpersonal relationships, both with classmates and close relatives, are often used to evaluate functional impairment – a prerequisite for ADHD diagnosis.

Optimizing the ADHD Brain for School

It's critical for children with ADHD to participate in physical activities that require them to move their bodies rather than just sitting and remaining in a calm, sedentary setting. Their brains execute cognitive

41

functions significantly better and more efficiently during physical activity. It's also unnecessary for the movement to be robust or encompass the whole body. Small motions might often be enough to get the job done. 'ADHD children can frequently be seen tapping their feet, nibbling on a pencil, or moving in their seats. To focus, their brains want movement.

Long stretches of work should be broken up into shorter sessions, with physical activity in between. Large assignments should be broken up into smaller ones.

Children need to consume the correct kinds of meals for brain health in addition to getting regular physical exercise and shorter instruction sessions. A diet high in protein and fiber is also vital. Caregivers need to avoid giving children processed foods and artificial sweeteners but rather focus on fresh, unprocessed whole foods.

ADHD in Adults

Adult ADHD may cause insecure relationships, poor job or school performance, poor self-esteem, and other issues. Even though it's termed adult ADHD, symptoms begin in childhood and often last throughout maturity. Adult ADHD symptoms may not be as apparent as those seen in children. Hyperactivity in adults may lessen, but impulsivity, restlessness, and difficulties paying attention may persist. While some individuals with ADHD have fewer symptoms as they age, others continue to have significant symptoms that interfere with everyday functioning. Adults with ADHD may have difficulties paying attention, impulsivity, and anxiety. The signs and symptoms might be moderate to severe.

Many adults with ADHD aren't even aware that they have it; all they know is that regular activities are challenging for them. Adults with ADHD may have trouble focusing and prioritizing, leading to missed deadlines and forgotten meetings or social activities. The inability to manage impulses may manifest in various ways, from restlessness when standing in a queue or driving in traffic to bouts of depression and angry outbursts.

Adult ADHD therapy is comparable to children's ADHD treatment. Medication, psychological counseling (psychotherapy), and treatment for any co-occurring mental health disorders are part of adult ADHD treatment.

The Negative Effects If Left Untreated

Because ADHD manifests itself in behavior, it is essential to understand how this disorder will affect the person living with ADHD and the others with whom they will interact. Family members, acquaintances, instructors, and classmates all experience the effects of ADHD daily. As a result, the first conclusion derived from this issue is that many individuals will be affected as long as the person with ADHD is left untreated. The consequences of not receiving treatment may be far-reaching for the person with the condition and those in their circle.

In terms of schooling, a kid with ADHD may struggle to pay attention in class and recall what little knowledge they have acquired. Consequently, the child may fall behind their class's average level.

Regarding social connections, the child may struggle to make and maintain friendships and relate to others. They may be seen as troublemakers who are not accepted in social situations. The most significant risk here is that the child develops feelings of being different and a poor self-image. This drives the child into a distinct area of psychosocial separation in addition to behavioral differentiation, which may lead to another set of issues that are much more significant and difficult to cure.

Adult ADHD, if left untreated, may also result in lasting problems. Adults with untreated ADHD may have impaired executive functioning, low self-esteem, and an increased risk of depression and anxiety. Adult ADHD may be addressed with the appropriate diagnosis and medication.

The Positive Aspects of ADHD

It is often disheartening to receive a diagnosis of ADHD for yourself or your child. While the condition causes negative issues like impulsive behavior and difficulty paying attention, it does have positive features. According to a survey of persons with ADHD, while hyperactivity (the inability to remain still) may be a bothersome sign of ADHD, they have, on average, greater energy levels than those without ADHD.

In addition, treatments that promote self-regulation are often used to treat ADHD. As a result, persons with ADHD discover their triggers and behaviors and how to regulate them more quickly than many neurotypicals. Individuals with ADHD learn how to calm and control themselves as part of their therapy, a skill many neurotypical people struggle with.

47

Additionally, those with ADHD have a greater risk tolerance than those who do not have the disorder. In some instances, this might be advantageous since it allows them to attempt alternatives that others would not.

In school, creative problem-solving is essential for academic and professional success. According to studies, those with ADHD have higher creativity and idea production levels than those without the disorder. This may lead to innovative thinking that comes from thinking outside the box. In addition, many persons with ADHD become hyper-focused on topics that they find interesting. This might result in meticulous attention to detail and a strong desire to complete school and job assignments that they find interesting.

Here are some additional positive aspects of someone with ADHD. Of course, these cannot be generalized to everyone.

- Optimistic, focused on the positive, and tends to forget negative aspects.
- Passionate about what motivates them
- Can achieve outstanding results by specializing in a specific area
- Sensitive and caring, especially regarding their families
- Sincere and honest
- Strong-willed. Although they have difficulties in school and other areas and feel misunderstood, they are distinguished by the fact that they quickly recover and are persistent in attempting to achieve their goals. They don't shy away from difficulties and tend to face them proactively.

- Ingenuous. They are usually creative and original people. Many have high levels of imagination, making it easy for them to develop creative skills.

- Energetic. Many need less sleep than others, and that hyperactivity can be channeled towards healthy lifestyle habits such as exercise and sport.

- Expert in solving problems. Their creativity and imagination make them capable of solving problems or situations differently from others, which is why they are considered great generators of ideas.

- Hyperfocused. This characteristic of ADHD is that while doing an activity, the person may be completely distracted or selectively focus all their attention on one detail. This, coupled with their passion and dedication to what they love,

can make them brilliant in some areas.

Ten Most Common Misconceptions about ADHD

Myth 1: Children with ADHD outgrow this condition.

Parents and many clinicians assumed that once children with ADHD reached adolescence and later maturity, their ADHD would go away. However, new research has shown that for as many as 85 percent of these children, certain features of ADHD might last far into adulthood. Adults who take ADHD medication for the remainder of their lives may still benefit from it. Others show enough progress that medications are no longer required, depending on their chosen profession and ability to thrive in relationships and other social activities. Many adults learn to modify their surroundings, maximize their abilities, and enjoy highly productive adult lives, even if their ADHD symptoms continue.

Myth 2: ADHD is caused by poor parental discipline.

Attention-deficit/hyperactivity disorder (ADHD) is not caused by a lack of parental discipline, although ADHD-related behaviors may make otherwise successful parenting techniques difficult. However, many established parenting approaches may assist children with ADHD in managing their behavior and provide structure and boundaries. However, inconsistent limit-setting and other inadequate parenting approaches might exacerbate it.

Myth 3: People with ADHD are usually hyperactive.

While hyperactivity is a symptom of ADHD, it is not the only symptom. There are many kinds of ADHD, including hyperactivity, inattentiveness, and a combination of the two.

People usually associate hyperactivity with ADHD because of its outward manifestations – short attention span, fidgeting, and frequent movement – however, hyperactivity may also be a less obvious symptom for many people as it is an internal issue for some. These individuals may seem quiet on the outside, but their thoughts are running at one hundred miles per hour in twenty-five different directions, making it hard to focus on a single idea or task.

Myth 4: ADHD medications lead to drug dependency.

Studies have revealed that the opposite is true. People who get effective ADHD treatment are LESS likely to develop a drug misuse issue than those who do not receive treatment. This is likely because people who do not seek assistance – whether via medication, behavioral therapy, or both – are more likely to experience anxiety and despair, leading to self-medication with illegal narcotics. On the other hand, medication is just ONE tool in a toolbox of options for treating ADHD. Behavioral therapy, diet, regular exercise, and other lifestyle modifications may help reduce symptom severity as well.

Myth 5: Everyone has a "'bit" 'of ADHD."

Having difficulties concentrating on occasion, or being a bit forgetful or disorganized, is not the same as having ADHD. Sure, everyone has problems with focusing now and again, but 'most people are probably quite neurotypical unless their concentration problems are affecting their life regularly. While it may seem that everyone has a little ADHD, people who make such claims devalue a whole population of people suffering from neurodevelopmental illnesses.

Myth 6: ADHD is "'all in your head.'"

While many people feel that ADHD is always a reason for children not concentrating or finishing their homework, this is not true. ADHD is, in a sense, in a person's head — or, more precisely, in their brain. According to research, specific brain areas in individuals with the illness don't coordinate correctly, and their general brain structure differs from that of persons who don't have it. That said, it is not "in someone's head" because they can't just snap out of it with a bit of self-discipline.

Persons with ADHD have brains that work differently than people who do not have ADHD. The posterior cingulate and medial prefrontal cortex do not match up in ADHD individuals, resulting in concentration issues. Other research has shown that specific brain connections are slower and less developed in ADHD patients, making it harder to concentrate on external activities.

Myth 7: ADHD is a condition that only children may have.

While the illness is more frequent in children and teenagers (the CDC estimates that 11 percent of American children aged 4 to 17 have ADHD), it also affects adults. Although children are more likely to be diagnosed, many people are diagnosed at the age of 30 or even later.

Myth 8: ADHD occurs only in boys

Although boys are twice as likely as girls to be diagnosed with ADHD, this does not mean girls are not diagnosed with it. This is said because boys tend to be more hyperactive than girls; this is probably so because girls tend to have more impulse control than boys.

Myth 9: If you have difficulties concentrating, you may have ADHD.

You don't necessarily have ADHD if you have difficulties concentrating, but it is a possibility. We all have concentration issues, and various factors such as anxiety, worry, sadness, sleep deprivation, and insufficient physical activity may contribute to them. To be diagnosed with ADHD, a child must exhibit six or more symptoms of inattention, and an adult must exhibit five or more, according to the DSM-5. Failure to pay attention to details, homework, or other duties, not listening when spoken to directly, and misplacing items important for school or other duties are just a few examples.

Myth 10: Attention deficit hyperactivity disorder (ADHD) is over-diagnosed.

While the number of reported ADHD diagnoses has increased since 1997, the CDC warns, "it is impossible to know whether this increase reflects a variation in the number of children with ADHD or a change in the number of children who were diagnosed." Many ADHD instances are believed to have gone undiagnosed until recently.

CHAPTER 2: WOMEN HAVE ADHD TOO!

New Hope for Women Struggling with ADHD

Women are more likely than males to be diagnosed with attention deficit hyperactivity disorder (ADHD) later in life. This is because women's symptoms vary from men's, and studies on the illness in women are limited. When women learn they have attention deficit

59

hyperactivity disorder, they often feel relieved (ADHD). They may have blamed themselves for their "faults" for years, and their self-esteem suffers. Emotional, mental, and bodily tiredness may have resulted from their intense anxiety over every facet of their life. Once they're' diagnosed with ADHD and know that their symptoms are not their fault, things seem to make more sense. Feelings of insecurity may melt away once individuals recognize they have ADHD, placing them in a stronger position to treat and deal with their symptoms.

If you have ADHD, you will know how it sometimes makes a person feel misunderstood and frustrated. However, it doesn't have to be an obstacle. Instead, try to learn as much as possible about this disorder and how to manage it. There is no quick fix for ADHD but know that you are not alone. If you use the strategies in this book and work with your doctors and therapists, you can figure out how to become the best version of yourself.

How to Recognize ADHD in Women

It's reported that 50 to 75 percent of female ADHD cases go undiagnosed. ADHD is commonly "hidden" in females since they develop differently than males, and males are much more prone to exhibit more overt and hyperactive symptoms of the illness. As a result, many girls grow into women who suffer quietly with their condition. Even after being diagnosed, people may be bewildered since their symptoms do not match those frequently reported while searching for ADHD information.

There are various reasons why a woman's ADHD diagnosis may be overlooked, most of which center on a misconception of how ADHD manifests distinctively in men and women. If you're an adult woman who believes you have ADHD or is bewildered by a recent diagnosis, here are four tips that will help you:

1. Find out what an ADHD diagnosis entails.

An official diagnosis of ADHD can be given by a mental health professional such as a psychologist or psychiatrist, or by a medical professional such as a pediatrician. You may meet with a physician to talk about your symptoms, how they influence you, and how long they've been bothering you. You may be asked to complete surveys or provide information on your upbringing and mental health. A medical exam may be performed to rule out specific medical conditions.

2. Look for the signs.

In general, females exhibit more significant signs of

inattention and less hyperactivity than men. Symptoms of Inattentive ADHD include not paying careful attention to detail; difficulty trying to hold attention to activities and tasks; trouble concentrating even on direct conversations. Others include the following:

- Difficulty following through on tasks such as schoolwork or projects; being easily sidetracked
- Difficulties with planning and scheduling
- Ignoring or disparaging tasks that involve attentiveness
- Losing things regularly
- Disorganization
- Low self-esteem
- Poor time assuming responsibilities
- Psychological distress
- Feelings of inadequacy

63

- Lack of attention to detail

- Difficulty with multitasking

- Bad temperament

- Anxiety

- Chronic stress

- Depression

- Constant exhaustion

- Difficulty sleeping

If you have had six or more symptoms of inattention for more than six months, a mental health professional may diagnose you with ADHD.

3. Recognize hyperactivity or impulsive symptoms.

Women are less likely to be diagnosed with ADHD than males because many ADHD women are not hyperactive, and many people mistake hyperactivity for an ADHD diagnosis. Some women, however, are also prone to impulsivity and hyperactivity. Your therapist may inquire about hyperactive symptoms and how long they have bothered you. Six or more of the following symptoms for at least six months are required for a diagnosis of ADHD (predominantly hyperactive-impulsive): Fidgeting, tapping feet, or often wriggling, leaving your seat regularly while being seated was required, having trouble conducting quiet tasks, chatting incessantly, disrupting others, and so forth.

4. Take note of how symptoms affect you.

To be diagnosed with ADHD, your symptoms must be causing you discomfort and interfering with your daily life. While many individuals misplace items or forget things easily, ADHD symptoms cause issues at school, at work, in the household, or with relationships.

Your physician or therapist may inquire about

symptoms you had as a child under 12. Identifying signs of inattention and impulsivity/hyperactivity before this age that impacted your behavior in numerous contexts, such as home, school, and social interactions, is required for an ADHD diagnosis.

How ADHD Differs in Women

ADHD is often overlooked in females since their symptoms may be less bothersome and do not always match the ADHD paradigm. Inattentive symptoms are more common in girls and women than hyperactivity/impulsivity. Internalizing symptoms are also more common than externalizing ones.

Girls, especially when younger, are typically capable of developing coping techniques that disguise their ADHD symptoms. When they display symptoms, they are often misdiagnosed with other illnesses like depression or anxiety (both of which are typical co-occurring conditions for girls and women with ADHD). Because the Diagnostic and Statistical Manual of Mental Disorders (DSM-5) was produced using primarily male samples, girls and women tend to satisfy fewer of the diagnostic criteria for ADHD when tested.

According to studies, teachers are much less likely to send females for ADHD testing than males, which may contribute to prolonged management and therapy. These gaps in management and therapy often obstruct fundamental abilities learned in early childhood, resulting in academic and psychological deficits in girls and women.

Symptoms of ADHD in girls and women may:

- Seem to be less intense in girls and women than in boys and men (but girls and women may still show hyperactive/impulsive symptoms)
- Become more apparent later, typically during periods of social or academic transition
- Be recognized by adult women, causing them to seek evaluation and treatment (rather than being referred)
- Be aggravated by hormonal fluctuations, such as adolescence, menstruation, pregnancy, and menopause.

How gender stereotypes influence the behavior of women with ADHD

When we mix menstruation, hormones, and all-too-common female stereotypes, it's no wonder women are more likely to confuse ADHD symptoms with everyday fatigue.

First of all, the most well-known type of ADHD is Hyperactive-Impulsive. This type usually shows symptoms such as feeling restless, talking excessively, and poor decision-making skills. Research shows that men are more likely to suffer from this type of ADHD. At the same time, women tend to have the inattentive type of ADHD and have many more internalized symptoms. This is in contrast to hyperactive ADHD, where impulsiveness and disorganization are often more visible. Those with inattentive ADHD can be seen as quiet or shy, which is why they may go unnoticed in social situations.

Secondly, ADHD symptoms in women are often explained as personality traits rather than ADHD. For example, a woman may be seen as distractible, a daydreamer, forgetful, or very talkative. As a result, years often pass before they seek help to improve their mental health.

69

Finally, most of these symptoms directly impact a person's self-esteem. Those suffering from this disorder can recognize frequent forgetfulness, inability to carry out their plans, daydreams in awkward situations, and lack of organization and planning. They also suffer from difficulty coping with work and fulfilling personal responsibilities on top of having a high susceptibility to anxiety. As a result, they may feel guilty and have to deal with stress or anxiety related to their overwhelming responsibility. This is all on top of the

social expectation that women must reconcile caring for children, household, and family with their other personal obligations.

Examples of Women with ADHD Who Are Thriving

1. Emma Watson

Emma Watson is a former United Nations Goodwill Ambassador and a Brown University alumna. She was diagnosed with combined type ADHD when she was a child. While Emma hasn't spoken publicly about her ADHD, the ADHD Foundation revealed in a Facebook post that she had been diagnosed and treated for it since she was a kid while shooting the *Harry Potter* films. Emma's diverse achievements in film and women's rights, as well as her unmistakable composure and elegance, remind us that women with ADHD can still achieve great things.

2. Solange Knowles

Solange Knowles is a gifted and successful woman who has also been diagnosed with ADHD. Solange admitted to News 24 that her disordered speech and excitement sometimes led others to believe she was high even though she was not. She also admitted to being skeptical about the ailment at first but later accepted her diagnosis and noticed that ADHD symptoms are common in Hollywood.

3. Paris Hilton

Paris Hilton was diagnosed with ADHD at a young age. She exhibited inattention symptoms, making it difficult to pay attention to what was happening around her. She took Adderall (a stimulant for the central nervous system) since she was 12, but until she spent 23 days in jail for a traffic infraction in 2007, she realized how difficult it was to live with the disease. She "learned how to live with" her ADHD, which never hindered her professional life.

4. Erin O'Connor

Erin O'Connor was diagnosed with ADHD when she was in her forties. The mother of two, now 43, believes the diagnosis has helped her understand some aspects of her life.

"I've realized that I have ADHD, which is new; in hindsight, being able to put everything together and understand certain aspects of my personality and development has been quite beneficial," she told Stella magazine earlier this year.

5. Simone Biles

Simone Biles is an American artistic gymnast who has won seven Olympic gold medals. She has been transparent about her ADHD and believes that taking medication for it while competing is not an unfair game. She emphasized, "Having ADHD and taking medication for it is nothing to be embarrassed by," and she wasn't hesitant to tell others about it. Simone wants to keep the conversation open so that people can see ADHD as a unique trait rather than a flaw or disorder that limits one's potential. In an interview with Understood, a nonprofit organization that offers online services for ADHD, Biles stated, "It's never held me back, and I never let it hold me back. I believe it all comes down to how you handle the learning impairment. If you make it seem like a problem, people will believe there is one."

As we can see, many women with ADHD are fighters who haven't let their diagnosis hold them back. Many individuals with ADHD operate exceptionally well with help and effort.

The Impact

The challenge for many females who have not been diagnosed is they may have to learn a range of (not always positive) compensatory strategies such as using alcohol or other substances to slow them down. Social interaction may be achieved with higher-risk activities.

Coping strategies may be less overtly noticed, such as avoiding specific events, settings, or people, not facing up to problems, spending too much time online, or not seeking out help when needed. Women with ADHD may experience challenges in the workplace, such as disorganization, inattention, difficulty accepting constructive criticism and appraisal, and difficulties managing interpersonal relationships with colleagues. Working longer hours (but often hidden from others) to complete tasks because of time management/focus challenges can also be exhausting. Cycles of burnout may also be more common but may not be recognized or seen as something else.

ADHD is linked to lower achievements academically and poorer employment levels, especially if the person has a history of numerous job changes. Consequently, persons with ADHD are more likely to have poor self-esteem and conviction. According to studies, people with ADHD are twice as likely to be jailed and get divorced, and they are less happy with their personal, social, and professional lives. The effects of ADHD have also been linked to an increase in significant traffic accidents. It's an illness that has brought tremendous misery to many individuals who have it as well as their family members, partners, friends, and coworkers.

Cultural Stigma

For a woman with ADHD, her most painful challenge may be a struggle with her overwhelming sense of inadequacy in fulfilling the roles she feels are expected of her by her family and by society. Both on the job and at home, women are often placed in the role of caretakers. While men with ADHD are advised to build a support system around themselves, not only do few women have access to such a support system, society had traditionally expected women to be the support system.

Women diagnosed with ADHD are more likely to struggle with segregation in their communities. They are often separated from others because they are different; they might also suffer attentional, organizational, and social difficulties.

Workplace

The struggles for women with ADHD have been intensified with the emergence of "dual career couples." During much of the past two decades more and more women have been required to not only fulfill most if not all of the more traditional roles of wife and mother, but also to function efficiently and tirelessly as they juggle the demands of a full-time career. Problems such as tardiness, high error rate, interpersonal conflict, high absenteeism, lack of

77

dependability, and inability to change might lead to various issues in their place of work which might make them look incompetent and even result in work termination.

School

People with ADHD find it difficult to focus on a given task which might cause difficulties in executing school or work projects. It can also limit their ability to study, which causes depression, stress, and anxiety.

Relationships

ADHD patients experience emotions excessively, which often seem overwhelming to them. They feel pain, joy, and anger intensely, which may lead to impulsive behaviors they regret later.

Day-to-Day Life

ADHD causes distraction and often makes one

forgetful; time management also becomes an issue because of the inability to focus. These may lead to sufferers mixing up dates for school, work, and other projects.

Get Evaluated

A variety of experts may make the diagnosis of ADHD. ADHD may be diagnosed by a psychotherapist, psychiatrist, psychoanalyst, neurologist, or certain physicians. Before scheduling a consultation, inquire about the provider's expertise in diagnosing ADHD. To get tested for ADHD, you should start by speaking with your family physician. They may not be able to provide you with a complete assessment, but they may be able to recommend you to someone who can. Many pediatricians and general practitioners are competent in diagnosing ADHD. If your doctor feels you or your child has the condition, you may request a referral to a specialist for a more thorough evaluation. Please remember – ADHD cannot be diagnosed over the internet. However, numerous online ADHD tests and questionnaires may be used as self-screening tools. A questionnaire might give you the confidence to seek a formal diagnosis from a health expert.

What is involved in a complete ADHD evaluation?

An ADHD evaluation has many goals: to determine if a person exhibits the symptoms that suggest ADHD, to determine whether the symptoms are severe enough to warrant a diagnosis, and to determine whether the person has more than one illness at the same time. The healthcare practitioner or ADHD expert will inquire about the following symptoms to determine if the person has ADHD symptoms: (i) Inattention, (ii) Impulsivity, and (iii) Hyperactivity.

Simply evaluating ADHD symptoms may be enough to get an ADHD diagnosis; however, this alone is often insufficient to assist a person in obtaining the appropriate therapy. All probable reasons for behavioral issues will be considered in a comprehensive examination. The complete evaluation will inquire about the child's or adult's conduct at home, school, work, and extracurricular activities such as sports. In the case of a child, the evaluation will include details from a child's parents or guardians, daycare providers, teachers, other school staff, or other mental health specialists.

As an adult, an initial meeting will be held to identify the problems you are experiencing. The doctor or specialist will want to know how your symptoms affect your daily life and why you want to be evaluated. They'll ask about your education and medical history to determine if you've had these symptoms throughout your life or if they only started showing up recently. A diagnosis of ADHD requires that the person has had at least some symptoms before age 12.

On the day of your appointment, you may be asked to complete one or more questionnaires or checklists designed to determine the frequency of ADHD-related behaviors. Your doctor may send them to you ahead of time for you to complete at home before the meeting.

A subsequent meeting will be scheduled to discuss the results and develop a plan. You and your doctor will also agree on how you will track your progress.

These are the three basic components of an evaluation for ADHD. However, the doctor or specialist usually focuses on different things depending on the age of the person being evaluated.

Online ADHD Assessment

Here are a couple of websites that you can check out to perform a quick online assessment: https://www.additudemag.com/self-test-adhd-symptoms-women-girls/

https://aschermd.com/self-test-women/

NOTE: This self-test is not intended to diagnose the condition or to replace the care of a health care professional. Only a doctor or mental health professional can diagnose ADHD based on a thorough clinical evaluation.

CHAPTER 3: UNMASKING THE BIAS

Why are Women with ADHD Underdiagnosed?

Women, particularly mothers, are the fastest increasing group of individuals diagnosed with ADHD. Male ADHD overshadows female ADHD; we know that males are three times more often than girls to be diagnosed with ADHD. However, women with ADHD do exist, and an estimated 50 to 75 percent of women with ADHD go undiagnosed. Males are more likely to exhibit hyperactive/impulsive conduct, a characteristic of ADHD. Many people are unaware that there is an inattentive variety of ADHD, which is the most frequent among females. Inattentive ADHD symptoms tend to go unnoticed in young girls, who may blend into their classes' backgrounds while daydreaming.

Males with ADHD are identified more often and earlier than females since their symptoms are more visible and dramatic. Lack of organization, forgetting or misplacing belongings, difficulties concentrating on a single job or activity, becoming quickly distracted, having multitasking issues, and unwillingness or aversion to activities requiring lengthy amounts of attention are all indicators of inattentive ADHD. Because most of these symptoms occur within the mind, they might be overlooked by families, patients, and mental health experts. However, more adult women are finding they have had untreated ADHD from childhood than ever before.

One reason women's ADHD stays misdiagnosed or undiagnosed is that current societal expectations of women are different, and the symptoms of the form of ADHD most typically observed in women match these expectations. For example, since society's expectations of females vary from boys', parents and instructors may not be concerned if a girl is a little unorganized, sloppy, or "in her own world." Things may worsen for women as they reach maturity and are expected to be more structured, possibly managing employment and family. Hormonal differences is another reason women's ADHD isn't adequately diagnosed. If women are "ditzy, inattentive, or impractical," hormones are blamed rather than digging into the cause of these issues.

Certainly, the female hormones produced throughout adolescence, the menstrual cycle, and menopause alter how ADHD symptoms appear. The amounts of dopamine and serotonin, for example, are reduced after menopause. Because these brain neurotransmitters are required for attention and mental alertness, women going through menopause often have difficulty completing activities and become easily side-tracked. These signs and symptoms are also typical in people with ADHD. So, typical female hormonal changes may be concealing the signs and symptoms of ADHD.

In 2016, the Centers for Disease Control and Prevention (CDC) estimated that 9.4 percent of children in the United States, or 6.1 million children, had been diagnosed with ADHD. Boys had more than twice the number of cases among this group compared to females.

In addition, according to the National Institute of Mental Health (NIMH), the lifetime incidence of ADHD is 8.1 percent in individuals aged 18 to 44. Men are still more likely than women to be diagnosed with ADHD, however, by a narrower margin of 5.4 percent to 3.2 percent. Based on various research findings, one can assume that women with ADHD aren't identified until maturity, when their symptoms may grow more severe.

Gender Differences in Research

Reports to the National Resource Centre on ADHD Children and Adults with ADHD (CHADD) show that there is little information about ADHD in women due to few studies being conducted on this population. Most of the information available is based on the clinical experience of mental health professionals who specialize in treating adult women.

This lack of information may be because women go undiagnosed as children, as they are more likely to go unnoticed and under-diagnosed due to the disorder's different symptomatic manifestations.

Due to a lack of research evidence, resources, and public awareness of the illness among females, women and girls with ADHD confront different obstacles. Due to social stigma, many girls and women with ADHD are afraid to speak out about their experiences.

It is important to emphasize that the difference between the sexes is not in the symptoms but in their different expression and influence on the functionality of men and women. The brain morphology is the same in both sexes, but the expression of the symptoms is very different since they manifest themselves as a function of the internalization of control over their daily activity.

Girls and women experience ADHD symptoms in various ways. A girl with ADHD may be less hyperactive and impulsive than her male counterpart, displaying milder symptoms. Instead of interrupting the class with excessive movement, her hyperactivity might be exhibited in other ways, such as constant drawing in the corners of her textbooks. She may also show her hyperactivity by conversing continuously, which could be mistaken for her merely being sociable. Girls are more likely than boys to have the inattentive and impulsive form of ADHD, which is often misdiagnosed as mood disorders, anxiety, and depression.

Girls with ADHD may go undetected because they work harder to disguise their symptoms than their male counterparts. To compensate for their difficulties, females are more likely to put in additional hours of studying and seek help from instructors. Girls are also more likely to be socialized to try everything possible to fit in, even if they are aware that they are "different" in some way. Lack of organization, disorientation, and difficulty focusing are common symptoms in females. She may look shy or aloof as an introvert who has social difficulties. Because she is often distracted, comprehending information may take her longer. Consequently, she may be misunderstood as sluggish or even incoherent, whereas in reality, she may be incredibly clever. She'll probably feel a lot of humiliation and inadequacy.

Statistics

- 4 out of 10 teachers report more difficulty in recognizing ADHD symptoms in girls than in boys (National Center for Gender Issues and ADHD).

- The fastest-growing population undergoing treatment for ADHD is adult women ages 24 to 36 (Kaleidoscope Society).

- By adulthood, most women with ADHD have at least one comorbid disorder that can complicate ADHD symptoms, including anxiety, bipolar disorder, and depression (National Comorbidity Survey Replication, *American Journal of Psychiatry*).

- Males are almost three times more likely to be diagnosed with ADHD than females (National Institute of Mental Health).

- It's estimated that as many as 50 to 75 percent of cases of ADHD in girls are missed (Healthline).

More Research is Necessary

Some doctors agree that more research on gender differences in ADHD is needed. Females may need therapy that differs from that required by boys and men. Female hormones, for example, are thought to have a role in the symptoms of ADHD in young girls and women, according to some specialists. Many females are also taught to act differently than guys. This may cause people to manifest their symptoms in different ways. Finally, specialists believe that additional research will aid in the early detection, diagnosis, and treatment of symptoms in young girls and women. Early intervention is critical for improved long-term treatment of the illness. More research can help increase education, remove stigma, and improve treatment for those who live with ADHD and are looking for help.

CHAPTER 4: CAN ADHD BE TREATED?

Medical Treatment

While ADHD cannot as yet be prevented or cured, it can be managed, and there are several treatment options. When an individual is diagnosed with ADHD, parents typically worry about the best remedy for their child. With an appropriate treatment and education plan, ADHD symptoms may be controlled. Several therapy options are available, and what works best for each child, adult, and family is unique. In the case of children, parents should collaborate with those engaged in their child's life, such as healthcare professionals, psychologists, instructors, trainers, and close relatives, to identify the best solutions and ensure everyone is on the same page. Common treatments used to manage ADHD include:

1. Behavioral intervention
2. Medications

Behavioral Interventions and Therapy

Behavioral interventions involve one of two kinds of ADHD treatment that have been proven to be successful. Behavioral therapy for children includes behavioral parent training (BPT), school instructional techniques, and executive function interventions. A child's age will decide which form of intervention to utilize, and critical concepts of behavior management apply across the many types of behavior intervention. BPT and school instructional techniques are often employed for younger children, but older children, including teenagers, are given techniques to deal with executive function issues. ADHD impairs a child's ability to pay attention and sit still in class, as well as their interactions with their family and peers. Children with ADHD often engage in actions that are disturbing to others. Behavior therapy is a therapeutic option that may lessen these behaviors; starting behavior therapy as soon as a diagnosis has been made is frequently beneficial. The objectives of behavior therapy are to develop or enhance beneficial habits while eliminating undesirable or troublesome behaviors.

For adults with ADHD, cognitive-behavioral therapy (CBT) is most often used. Simply put, this therapy helps you change how you behave by changing how you think. It targets unhelpful thought processes and replaces them with helpful ones. It helps you to see things in a more balanced light. For instance:

- All or nothing thoughts such as "I was turned down for that job interview. I'll never get a job." This can be replaced with, "Sure, I was turned down for that interview. I'll apply for a more suitable position until something turns up."

- Focusing on the negative such as "I can't cope with work projects and household chores. I'm a terrible homemaker and employee." This can be replaced with, "I struggled this week, but at least I finished that important project before the deadline even if we had to get takeaways for dinner all week."

- Being overly dramatic such as "I made a stupid remark to my date about his car last night. He's definitely never going to contact me again."

- Personalizing everything such as "I'm the one who quoted on that big contract. If we lose the client, I'll be the one to blame." This can be seen instead as, "Yes, I quoted on the project, but the boss signed off on it, and Jerry talked with the client. At least we can take the knock as a team."

Medications

The administration of drugs to treat ADHD is the most successful in reducing the primary symptoms of the types of this disorder. The US Food and Drug Administration (FDA) has licensed various ADHD drugs, including stimulants (methylphenidate- and amphetamine meds) and non-stimulants (atomoxetine and antihypertensive meds, majorly the alpha-2 adrenergic agonists).

- **Stimulants**: While it may sound counterintuitive to use stimulants, this class of medicines has been used to successfully manage ADHD for years. These drugs may assist you in focusing your attention and ignoring distractions. 70% to 80% of patients benefit from stimulant medications. They're prescribed to those with moderate to severe ADHD. They may benefit children, teenagers, and adults who have difficulties at school, work, or home. Some stimulants are safe to use in children beyond the age of three. Others are suitable for youngsters above the age of six.

- **Non-stimulants**. Non-stimulants may aid when stimulants don't seem effective or if stimulant drugs have unpleasant side effects. These drugs may help with symptoms such as attention deficits and impulsive behavior.

- **Antidepressants**: Distress, stress, and bipolar illness are common in people with ADHD. They may take an antidepressant for these as well as a stimulant for ADHD to treat mental health disorders or other diseases.

Stimulants vs. Non-Stimulants

Non-stimulants are not the same as stimulants. However, some of the differences may be explained in terms of (i) how fast they begin to act, and (ii) the possible side effects.

1. **How fast they begin to act**

Stimulants usually take action quickly; a youngster might feel the benefits within 30 to 90 minutes of taking them. Stimulants exit the system in 3 to 12 hours, depending on the kind of stimulant – extended-release, immediate-release, or sustained release –and how a child reacts to them. The time it takes for an individual to observe symptom alleviation with non-

103

stimulants varies. It may take several days for some people instead of hours. Non-stimulants tend to last longer in the body than stimulants and may last up to 24 hours in the body.

2. **The possible side effects**

ADHD drugs – both stimulants and non-stimulants – have the potential for adverse effects, as do other medications. The following are some of the most frequent stimulant adverse effects: insomnia, lack of appetite, restlessness, jitteriness, tics, migraines, gastrointestinal problems, and racing pulse. Lethargy, reduced appetite, exhaustion, nausea, vomiting, sleeplessness, and agitation are all possible adverse effects of non-stimulants.

The most often given drugs for ADHD are stimulants. They're often the initial line of therapy for ADHD. This family of pharmaceuticals is known as central nervous system (CNS) stimulant medications. They function by boosting dopamine and norepinephrine levels in the brain. This action enhances focus while reducing the tiredness many people with ADHD experience.

Amphetamines, methamphetamines, and methylphenidate are all examples of stimulant medications. The majority are taken in oral pill form once or twice daily. These medications are also available in immediate-release, extended-release, and controlled-release oral dosage forms.

Non-stimulants have a different effect on the brain than stimulants. These medications also affect neurotransmitters, although they do not raise dopamine levels. In general, these medicines take longer to produce effects than stimulants.

There are various types of these medications. When stimulants aren't safe or effective, or if a person wishes to prevent the adverse effects of stimulants, a doctor may prescribe them. Atomoxetine, clonidine, and guanfacine ER are examples.

Atomoxetine works by preventing norepinephrine reuptake in the brain, prolonging its action. The medication is taken once or twice a day in an oral form. Clonidine ER is used to lower hyperactivity, impulsivity, and inattentiveness. Adults with high blood pressure are usually administered guanfacine. This medication may aid in the treatment of cognitive and behavioral issues. It may also aid in the reduction of hostility and hyperactivity.

Side Effects of ADHD Medication

Side effects are often a possibility with medications. Not everybody will have the same ones, and some
106

people will have none. Some side effects fade after a time of being on the medication, while others persist. Insomnia, lack of appetite, repetitive behaviors, mood swings, headaches, nausea, rebound effect, and an elevated heart rate and pulse are just a few of the adverse effects. It's important to discuss the drug's exact side effects with your physician and let them know if you experience any. They may adjust the dose or change to another medication.

Alternative Treatments

Some alternative treatment methods have been scientifically validated and demonstrated to be relatively beneficial in alleviating ADHD symptoms in investigations. These are some of them:

- **Exercise:** You've probably heard that physical activity produces hormones that may help to improve mood. It may also help children with

107

ADHD to pay attention. Dopamine, serotonin, norepinephrine, and GABA are some brain chemicals that exercise produces. Such neurotransmitters are often deficient in children with ADHD. Your child does not necessarily need to participate in a structured program to reap its benefits. Twenty minutes of press-ups, racing up and down stairs, or taking a quick stroll may suffice. According to the study, a 30-minute exercise session helped with executive function activities, including planning and prioritizing. Exercise is just as beneficial for adults with ADHD. Even a single exercise session can help you be more motivated for mental activities, provide focused energy, and reduce confusion. Exercise acts on your brain in much the same way as your medication. To gain the most benefit from exercise though, it's essential to find an activity that suits your lifestyle and that you enjoy, then do it regularly. This is because exercise's effects only last for a short time, like medication. You can think of your exercise session as a treatment dose that should be taken five days a week for 30 minutes each time.

- **Going outside**: Kids use their "voluntary" attention while completing schoolwork or cleaning their rooms. To put it another way, concentration requires work. Children with ADHD have trouble maintaining their focus. They may change to "involuntary" focus and obtain a much-needed break by spending quality time outdoors, particularly in a natural environment. In automated tasks, this kind of attention is required. Breathing and moving out of the path of falling items are examples. Children are not required to think about anything in particular. They may be better able to execute activities that need them to concentrate after taking a break from their voluntary concentration.

Adults with ADHD also benefit from time spent outdoors. It may be helpful to combine the exercise component of therapy with outdoor time by doing activities such as walking in the forest, hiking, or swimming in the ocean.

- **Omega supplements**: Some people with ADHD have been shown to have relatively low levels of omega fatty acids. These fatty acids aid in the communication of neurons in the brain. A lack of this communication might cause

ADHD-like symptoms. Omega fatty acids are found in foods such as fish, nuts, flaxseed, and some vegetables. Supplements containing them are also available. According to studies, people with ADHD who took these supplements showed a slight improvement in their symptoms.

- **Dietary changes:** Allergies and dietary sensitivities are more common in children with ADHD. Certain foods might impact their behavior and exacerbate their ADHD symptoms. Parents may seek food and nutrition counseling to discover whether dietary changes would be beneficial. ADHD adults and children alike would do well to cut out refined sugar, high-fructose corn syrup, food containing artificial colorants, flavorings, preservatives, and most processed foods. This change does not even require a doctor's consultation. Switching to a more whole-food, nutritious diet will improve everyone in the family's health, even if you don't witness a decrease in hyperactive behavior.

- **Melatonin:** ADHD often causes people to have trouble falling asleep. Melatonin is often promoted as a natural solution; some parents use it to help their children settle down and fall asleep.

CHAPTER 5: ADHD MANAGEMENT STRATEGIES

Multidisciplinary Approach for ADHD

A multidisciplinary approach to clinical diagnosis gathers information from experts and doctors with many experiences and specializations to offer a complete diagnosis. The following are some frequent areas of multidisciplinary evaluation:

- Psychology: This involves examining a child's developmental capabilities and obstacles, as well as any issues resulting from underlying behavioral, emotional, or cognitive problems.

- Communication: An evaluation by a licensed therapist might reveal developmental speech or language impairments, such as language processing abnormalities, articulation delays, and social language and psycholinguistics.

- Physical Therapy: A physical therapist may assist a child or even an adult with developing and strengthening gross motor skills like jogging, strolling, and jumping, which are necessary for health and to fulfill everyday activities and routines.

Collaborative Models in ADHD Management

A recent study by researchers showed that a "collaborative care" approach, which employs a "care manager" to act as a liaison between parents and clinicians, was more beneficial than a traditional pediatrician-centered strategy in treating ADHD in children.

The care manager will be in charge of gathering medical histories and symptom reports from families, as well as engaging with parents, pediatricians, and a specialist panel of child psychiatrists. A suitable care manager can break down barriers by addressing parents according to their level and discussing the ins and outs of an ADHD diagnosis and how correct treatment may improve their child's life.

If we want to increase positive behavior, we must associate it with a reward, prize, or praise (positive reinforcement, tangible or intangible reward). This works if the child has control over their actions.

However, some children have a predisposition to easy frustration for various reasons. It can be due to depression, anxiety, language difficulties, cognitive inflexibility, low IQ, cognitive and affective impulsivity (frequently associated with ADHD and Oppositional Defiant Disorder (ODD), or Dissocial Behaviour (CD)). In these children, the reward-punishment will not work. The punishment will frustrate them more and will worsen their explosiveness. Some children react very badly to changes in routine or have a hard time transitioning between activities.

These children have what is called an "Adaptive Skills Disorder," and any frustration, or situation that does not go exactly as they want it to go, will generate a very intense affective response – an effective explosion. A fundamental part of the treatment of ODD and CD is the training of parents in behavior modification techniques and behavioral management. This training aims to encourage positive behaviors and ignore negative behaviors when possible. Some important measures in which parents are trained are giving orders and using more effective punishments, establishing clear limits that should not be negotiated (few), and establishing other, less important rules on which there is room for negotiation.

Greene's model states that for those children with difficulty in adaptive skills it is also important to learn to detect those situations that can trigger disproportionate outbursts of aggressiveness in the child or adolescent to try to avoid them. It is especially important to prioritize our demands on the child. To prioritize, Greene divides situations into three types: A, B, and C.

• Type A situations. These are important and

potentially dangerous situations if the child doesn't obey, like crossing the street without looking or sticking their fingers into an electric socket. In these cases, the parents must impose their rule, even if this causes an explosion in the child.

• Type C situations. Some situations that are neither important nor dangerous (tidying up the room, finishing dinner) yet generate a lot of explosiveness in the child if we try to impose our criteria. It is better to let the child get away with it in these cases. It is not worth risking a hugely explosive situation for a small matter.

• Type B situations. Finally, some situations are neither important nor dangerous but are not minor either. Here, parents must negotiate with their child and find solutions that satisfy everyone. This type of training is usually effective because it greatly reduces explosive and violent reactions to situations.

Parents do not have to control everything, but only those behaviors that are important and dangerous. They have to make an effort to negotiate B-Type situations, to arrive at realistic and mutually satisfactory solutions.

Behavioral Intervention

It is essential to determine the target behavior before building a behavior management strategy. When deciding which behavior to change, keep the following evaluation concerns in mind:

- What is the child's functional level – what *can* they do?

- Is the child's conduct interfering with their goals?

- Whose life quality are you attempting to improve?

- Will you be able to keep track of the behavior to see whether it improves?

Several behavior management approaches may be tried; however, the first step must be to define the behavior's function (or to determine why the child behaves the way they do). Disruptive behavior might be used for several purposes, such as learning positive rewards, negative reinforcement, or learning stimulation/sensory control. In the case of children with ADHD, the behavior is more likely to be perpetrated by either positive reward, such as looking for attention from classmates or an adult/teacher, or negative reinforcement, such as escaping from an activity or task. If the disruptive conduct is driven by a desire to escape, altering the activities or giving the child an option may be enough to stop the behavior. Each child will need a specific intervention strategy.

School Strategies and Study Skills for Individuals with ADHD

Here are some common unhelpful methods that ADHD students employ to get their schoolwork done. We discuss better alternatives.

1. Preparing for exams through cramming

Students should spread their study sessions evenly to prevent cramming a lot of information a few hours before the exam. When we acquire ideas and knowledge in many spaced-out periods, we are better able to remember them. In the long term, several 30-minute study sessions spread out over many days are more beneficial than a three-hour crash course the night before. Consider an overloaded suitcase – the instant you move it, items will tumble out.

2. Seldom reviewing notes

Many ADHD kids and adolescents make the mistake of quickly skimming over their materials and assuming they're prepared for the test. The importance of repetition cannot be overstated. Read and reread for excellent studying retention.

3.   Rereading only

Rereading alone isn't going to help the child remember what they've read. Because the content is familiar, students may adopt a false "I know this!" approach while reviewing. They stop thinking about what they're reading and don't get a more profound knowledge of the content. Rewriting notes is a cure for this. Compared to reading the same content repeatedly, the physical act of writing helps pupils absorb knowledge on a deeper level. To take it a step further, have them rewrite in a different format to the original notes (draw a graphic, make an outline, design a Q&A — anything that modifies the structure of the notes). Students can determine if they genuinely comprehend the content by reorganizing the information.

4.   Only using one study tool

Regretfully, creating a single study guide will not suffice. Using various study tools can help the student learn more effectively by keeping the content new, enjoyable, and engaging.

5.   Ignoring practice questions

Most textbooks contain practice questions, but most students don't know that these questions are gold! But only if they put them to good use. It's advisable to write these questions before reading the textbook. It will help the child to take note of some essential points in the textbook. Many students find this simple strategy exceedingly helpful.

Management Strategies for Emotional and Social Issues

There are methods to regulate the emotional responses ADHD causes, but children may need additional assistance in knowing how to do so. Most individuals consider attention issues and fidgetiness when thinking of ADHD symptoms. They don't typically consider issues with emotion regulation. You may help your child develop emotional resistance by being a supportive parent and teaching them how to regulate their emotional responses.

1. Self-awareness

Consciousness and emotional awareness are two types of self-awareness that may assist persons with ADHD in regulating their emotions. Consciousness aids in the identification of harmful sentiments and the elimination of the emotional merry-go-round. Most significantly, children need to be taught to identify their feelings as they get inundated, to help them develop emotional awareness. Because emotions are so complicated, they should be asked to express how they're feeling using more than one word. This teaches children to identify their many emotions and how to respond to each one.

2. Develop coping techniques

Having a plan for dealing with emotional outbursts will immensely assist you and your child in dealing with them. Anticipating and planning for typical stresses is one method to deal with them. For instance, you may plan ahead of time if your youngster becomes upset while going to the grocery shop. You may plan to keep your shopping trip short, attempt to make it more fun and inventive, or do it as usual and afterward let your child play or watch their favorite program if they behave well. Everyday stresses should hopefully create less emotional anguish by using this method.

3. Develop a sense of gratitude

Redirecting emotions is one technique to help your child develop emotional resilience. To begin, encourage your youngster to replace the bad feeling with a happy one. Gratitude is a particularly effective antidote to bad feelings.

4. Seek life coaching/therapy to gain a better understanding of common stressors

You and your child might benefit from life coaching or counseling to learn how to better cope with emotional outbursts. A professional can show you how to deal with your child's tantrums effectively without further triggering or supporting their behavior. Your child's emotions may also be managed and appropriate coping methods implemented with the aid of a professional. Finally, a life coach or therapist may assist you and your child with identifying reoccurring stressors and determining if they can be eliminated or reduced in your child's life.

ADHD may heighten emotions and make it difficult for your child to function appropriately in society.

However, if you educate your child to be self-aware, alert, and prepared, they will be able to develop emotional resistance early on and be more equipped to deal with future stress.

Managing Your Time

Adults with ADHD tend to think about time differently than neurotypicals. Many cannot anticipate future rewards and consequences, procrastinate, and cannot stay focused. This causes issues with deadlines, punctuality, and planning. Here are several strategies experts recommend for helping you manage your time and concentrate on your tasks in the most efficient, effective, and happy way.

- **Keep a detailed daily schedule.** Take a couple of minutes at the start of your day to plan your priorities.

127

- **Use a planner.** Use a calendar or a day planner for your daily schedule, and to-do lists. Try different types of planners – digital, physical, or large calendars, and stick with the one that best works for you.

- **Break large tasks into smaller chunks.** When you have too much on your plate, it can feel overwhelming. However, if you break down big projects into manageable chunks, they can feel more doable and may even help you preserve your attention

- **Prioritize.** Write down your tasks and your to-do lists and order them by priority.

- **Make sleep, diet, and exercise a priority** since these will give you more energy and allow you to use your time more effectively.

- **Set timers and alarms.**

- **Limit distractions.** Turn off your phone volume when focusing on a task. Wear noise-canceling headphones if it is impossible to work in a quiet place.

Managing Stress

Having ADHD often means living with increased stress or processing stress in unique ways. The ADHD symptoms, such as trouble focusing, disorganization, and forgetfulness, can get in the way of practical problem-solving, managing emotions, or feeling in control of one's life. These difficulties can set the stage for feeling overwhelmed, discouraged, or even depressed. Research shows high rates of stress, family or marital conflict, academic or job underachievement, and financial challenges in ADHD patients. Overall, ADHD is a risk factor for chronic stress, and chronic stress often makes having ADHD more challenging.

If you have ADHD and are feeling a great deal of stress because of it, there are ways to manage it.

- Medication or therapy
- Engage in regular exercise or physical activity
- Spend time outdoors in nature
- Use tools to help you stay organized
- Take breaks throughout the day to decrease the chances of becoming overstimulated
- Keep your environment organized
- Practice relaxation and meditation techniques. Regular meditation and mindfulness practices help train your attention and help you to focus better.
- Get plenty of sleep
- Take pride in the things you do well. ADHD is just a part of you – it should not define you.

Managing Money

Adults with ADHD are prone to wasting money due to impulsiveness or an inability to handle details. Bookkeeping, checking books, and paying bills can be especially difficult for people with ADHD. Following this premise, Itzhak Ben-David, Professor of Finance at the Ohio State University Fisher College of Business, has led a study on the financial behavior of adults with ADHD. Ben-David surveyed 544 adults with the disorder, asking them about their debt management, employment history, and credit card use. The survey result showed that people with ADHD had difficulties both in the workplace and with personal finances, in both cases due to their tendency toward impulsive behavior.

"They live in the moment, and it is difficult for them to plan and think about the future," Ben-David pointed

131

out. The survey subjects were asked about their preference between taking $120 in a week or waiting a year and getting up to twice that amount, and the majority preferred the most present option.

If you have ADHD, you need to bite the bullet and create a budget. Don't let boredom or impulsiveness dig you into a huge financial hole. Your plan will depend on your income, the present state of your finances, your age, and your lifestyle. Here are five tips for getting started on a budget:

1. **Identify your problem areas.** These could include bouncing checks, losing bills, making impulsive purchases, or having large credit card balances. Identifying the situations when you manage your money poorly is the first step to coming up with solutions.

2. **Set short-term and long-term goals.** Do you want to bring down your credit card debt, save for an important large purchase, or build up an emergency fund? Make a list of your top priorities, then figure out how to accomplish them in small but measurable steps.

3. **Stay organized.** Use simple ledgers and folders labeled by the month for paid and unpaid bills. Open all your bills as soon as you get them, and program monthly payment reminders into your phone or computer. If you have trouble keeping track of your bills, consider automating your payments. You can also do your banking online so you have one place where you can find all your deposits, payments, and balances.

4. **Avoid impulse spending.** Giving in to your impulses may seem like fun, but it's an

important behavior to learn to control, especially regarding your money. Keep only one credit card, and when you shop, only bring the amount of cash you can afford to spend. Always use a shopping list and try as best as possible to stick to it.

5. **Track spending.** One of the most important financial tasks we face is to control daily spending. You don't need to keep detailed records or make complex calculations as there are many apps around today that will help you to track your spending easily and quickly. Think of it as just a way of finding out where your money is going.

CHAPTER 6: ADHD'S EFFECT ON RELATIONSHIPS

Attention Deficit Hyperactivity Disorder (ADHD) characteristics such as inattentiveness, disorganization, and impulsivity may negatively influence many aspects of life. Still, the symptoms of ADHD can be especially troublesome in relationships. Miscommunication, irritation, and displeasure may wreak havoc on personal relationships when one or both partners have ADHD. The good news is that understanding how ADHD impacts your relationship may help you establish methods and techniques to better communicate with your partner and, consequently, build a more robust, pleasant relationship.

How Does ADHD Affect Your Partner?

If your partner is diagnosed with ADHD, you may encounter recurrent misunderstandings and conflicts due to the symptoms. It generally happens when a problem goes untreated or is poorly handled. Here are a few ways that ADHD may impact your relationship to assist you in grasping the function of ADHD in adult relationships:

1. Dating with hyperfocus

When a partner has ADHD, it makes the other partner the focus of their existence throughout the early stages of dating and relationships; this is known as hyperfocus dating. This, however, does not endure long owing to ADHD. When hyperfocus fades and a connection develops, the ADHD partner's focus changes to something else. Because they don't receive the same treatment and attention as when the relationship began, the non-ADHD spouse may feel overlooked, uncared for, or unloved. A person with ADHD may be unaware that they have ceased paying attention to their spouse or the essential components of their relationship.

2. Parent-child-type relationships

One of the significant impacts of ADHD is that one person feels obligated to care for the ADHD partner, resulting in parent-child-type interactions. In the partnership, the ADHD person takes on the role of the irresponsible kid, while the non-ADHD partner takes on the role of the responsible parent. These dynamics may be harmful since the ADHD person feels trapped and controlled, while the other partner feels overwhelmed by having to handle everything.

3. Consistent debates

ADHD people are impulsive and prone to emotional outbursts. Consequently, they may make statements without considering the sentiments of others, resulting in disagreements. They tend to not be very diplomatic! Unmet expectations and conflicts owing to the partner's forgetfulness, carelessness, and rash actions may also lead to arguments. It might be challenging to talk about problems with your relationship when there are regular squabbles and emotional outbursts.

4. Symptom misinterpretation

When one partner has ADHD, symptom misunderstanding is to be expected in a relationship. It frequently happens when you believe you and your partner are well acquainted. As a result, when an ADHD spouse behaves in a specific manner, such as not paying attention to the person they love, it may seem like they are indifferent. Misinterpreting ADHD symptoms may lead to a blame game in which the ADHD partner seems to be the primary source of all the relationship issues.

Tips for Increasing Understanding in Your Relationship

Understanding ADHD in adult relationships might help you develop a great connection. Here are some suggestions for improving understanding in your relationship:

1. Learn all you can about ADHD.

The first step in gaining a better understanding of your partner is to educate yourself on ADHD. Knowing how the disorder presents in adulthood can allow you to approach your relationship issues in a new way. You'll not only figure out what's causing your partner's behavior but also learn how to respond differently.

Then you can figure out how to make your relationship work.

2. Communicate with your partner.

While ADHD may lead to miscommunication, developing good communication skills can help you and your partner understand each other better. You can address underlying reasons for tension and promote understanding in your relationship through effective communication. You may accomplish this by talking to each other as often as possible, meeting in person (try not to communicate about important issues over social media), avoiding the blame game by utilizing "I" words, and hearing your spouse out. Also, avoid having conversations while your emotions are running high.

3. Educate your partner about ADHD and how it affects you.

Your partner may feel anger and resentment toward an

ill-kept house or badly-behaved children, assuming that you "just don't care." He needs to appreciate the full brunt of ADHD's impact upon you. Get him on your side, strategizing about ways to make your life at home more ADHD-accommodating, and ADHD-friendly.

4. Concentrate on the positive aspects of your relationship.

Consider what made you fall in love with your spouse first, and attempt to do the same things you did when you were dating. Also, rather than concentrating on your partner's flaws, concentrate on their positive qualities and support them without making them feel childish. While ADHD may be detrimental to many relationships, most individuals with the disorder also have good characteristics, including cheerfulness, flexibility, perseverance, sympathy, and friendliness.

5. Exhibit empathy.

Recognize that having ADHD may have an impact on your relationship, regardless of who has it. If you have the disorder, you should understand how it impacts your relationship and sympathize with your spouse. If your spouse has ADHD, try to understand how tough it is to live with it. Separate your partner's personality from the disorder. You will be able to work on your relationship with joint effort and improve your understanding if you do so.

6. Seek help and treatment.

Treatment is the most effective approach to discovering a long-term solution to ADHD. Seek expert help as soon as you discover symptoms to ensure that the problem is addressed early in the relationship. This can help you control the symptoms and reduce the adverse effects of ADHD on your relationship. It would be best if you explored couples counseling in addition to individual ADHD treatment to help you overcome your relationship issues and develop a happy and healthy connection with your spouse.

ADHD Symptoms That Affect Your Relationship

Knowing which ADHD symptoms may impact your relationship gives you a better understanding of your partner's actions. It also enables you to connect your partner's actions and the condition. The following are some of the symptoms of ADHD that might lead to relationship issues:

- Risky conduct and impulsivity
- Lack of organizational skills
- Inattentiveness
- Emotional outbursts
- Lack of concentration
- Tardiness

143

- Difficulty taking direction or following procedures

You will be better positioned to address relationship issues if you understand the signs of ADHD that might trigger them.

A Short Message from the Author

Hi, are you enjoying the book thus far? I'd love to hear your thoughts! Many readers do not know how hard reviews are to come by, and how much they help an author.

I would be incredibly thankful if you could take just 60 seconds to write a brief review, even if it's just a few sentences!

Thank you for taking the time to share your thoughts!

CHAPTER 7: MANAGING CHILDREN

Tips for Parents of an ADHD Child

Is your kid suffering from ADHD? Learn how to cope with typical ADHD difficulties and control their behavior. Here are four (4) suggestions that may be useful:

Tip 1: Maintain a good attitude and a healthy lifestyle. As a parent, it's part of your job to create a healthy, happy, loving environment for your child's mental and physical well-being. Many of the elements that might benefit your child's disorder symptoms are under your control. Keep an optimistic frame of mind. Your positive attitude and common sense are your most vital assets for assisting your kid in dealing with the problems of ADHD. You are more willing to interact with your kid when you are relaxed and concentrated, which will assist him or her in being peaceful and remaining engaged.

Tip 2: Create a plan and stick to it.

When activities occur in regular rhythms and predictable settings, children with ADHD are more likely to complete them. Your role is to establish and maintain discipline and routines in your home so your child understands what to expect at certain times and how to behave in various situations.

148

Tip 3: Make time for movement and sleep.

Children with ADHD have a lot of energy to expend. Competitive sports and other fitness exercises help kids to healthily channel their enthusiasm and energy while also allowing them to concentrate on particular motions and hone their abilities. Physical exercise has several advantages, including improved focus, reduced sadness and stress, and increased brain development. Fitness leads to improved sleep, which in turn helps alleviate the symptoms of ADHD, which is essential for children with attention difficulties. Choose a sport that your kid will love and is a good fit for their abilities.

Tip 4: Establish clear expectations and guidelines.

Children with ADHD need rules that are clear and easy to follow. Make the family's norms of conduct basic and unambiguous. Make a list of the rules and post them somewhere your child may readily see them. Children with ADHD react exceptionally effectively to well-organized incentive and punishment systems. It's critical to clarify what will happen if the rules are followed and if they are disobeyed.

If you as a parent also have ADHD, you must understand and accept its challenges and identify your personal strengths and weaknesses. Identify sources of stress in your daily life and make systematic life changes to reduce them. For example, if the morning rush to get ready for work and school is a particularly stressful and challenging time, establish a routine of setting out clothing, breakfast, and so on the night before.

Prioritize your own needs and tasks and then you will be in a better position to help your child. Find structure and support from family and friends. Do not be afraid to ask significant others such as grandparents for help with child minding, for instance.

Foster a positive, effective, collaborative family climate with a fair division of responsibilities and emotional support. It's important that your child helps with chores and learns to shoulder some of the household responsibilities such as keeping their own bathroom tidy and clean as they get older.

Plan daily withdrawal periods for yourself. Soaking for half an hour in a warm bath is a great time to do this. Channel excess energy, anxiety, and negative emotions through leisure, sports, artistic activities, etc. Develop healthy self-care habits such as sleep hygiene, good nutrition, and a regular exercise routine.

How to Manage Your ADHD Teen

Teens with ADHD face the same concerns and challenges as their peers but with the added burden of their disorder. This is the age in which they continue to develop their identity. At this time, the principles of more independent functioning are established such as learning to manage money. Teens are trying to make sense of their emerging sexuality and have to make decisions regarding drugs and alcohol. On top of all this, they are dealing with school or college and setting their goals for the future. These tasks are challenging for any teen but adolescents with ADHD may face additional difficulties in successfully navigating them.

Adolescents with ADHD usually need more support and monitoring from their parents than usual. Even if your son or daughter was diagnosed in childhood and therefore knows of resources to manage their disorder, adolescence will present new challenges.

Adolescents with ADHD may experience feelings of shame and marginalization related to the diagnosis of their disorder. They may even refuse to accept that they have ADHD because they don't want to be different from their peers. They want to believe that their symptoms have disappeared with age and that they have "outgrown" them. The parents of adolescents must help them to recognize that the disorder exists and that it is a reality to be managed. Only then can the family begin to normalize the situation.

Motivating them to participate in the activities and skills that they enjoy and where they feel sure of themselves can be essential to helping them face and overcome the worries that their disorder brings about in them.

Meal Management

Although food is not a direct cause of attention deficit disorder, it may and can influence your child's mental state. This, in turn, influences their behavior. ADHD symptoms may be reduced by tracking what, when, and how much food your teen consumes. Teens are known for not eating regularly but "snacking" and this is even more the case with ADHD kids. Without parental supervision, these youngsters may go for hours without eating and then gorge on whatever is available. The physical and mental health of the person may be jeopardized as a consequence of this practice. Schedule frequent healthy meals or refreshments less than 3 hours apart to avoid dangerous eating patterns. On a physical level, regular mealtimes provide nourishment, and on an emotional level, they provide a much-needed respite from daily activities and a predictable pattern to the day.

154

For any teen, following a balanced diet is synonymous with good growth and performance, both academically and in sports. If they also have ADHD, special attention must be paid to their diet since they tend to forget that they have to eat and hydrate properly and often binge on sugary treats or nutrient-deficient snacks. According to a study by Yale University, if children with ADHD – hyperactive children, in particular –go on a sugar binge, they experience a rapid rise in adrenaline that causes hyperactivity. Establishing a meal schedule and guiding a varied and balanced menu is essential.

On the other hand, we must consider the decrease in appetite that pharmacological treatment for ADHD can cause, so we must emphasize breakfast and dinner. Enrich the diet with omega-three and omega-six fatty acids, which are beneficial for the brain and have to be taken externally since the body does not manufacture them. These components are found in sardines, salmon, tuna, nuts, and pumpkin.

Introduce foods rich in tryptophan, an amino acid precursor to serotonin, the so-called "sleep chemical". For example, chicken, milk, nuts, or sesame seeds.

The teen should be given foods rich in zinc and vitamin B6, necessary to synthesize serotonin together with tryptophan. For example, pate, figs, seafood, cereals, red meat, and chicken.

Teach them to avoid frequent stimulants such as drinks with caffeine and theine, chocolate, etc. They need to hydrate properly – the best drink is water, followed by milk beverages. Remember that even

100% natural fruit juices contain large amounts of sugar so if they are used, they should be diluted. An average of a liter and a half or two liters a day of water is recommended, increasing its consumption in summer.

Secrets to Stop Burnout for the ADHD Mum

Raising a child or teen with ADHD is full of challenges and frustrations. Let us remember that it is challenging for those with ADHD to concentrate on tasks, pay attention, stay still and control their impulsive behavior, which can cause intense exhaustion in both the mind and the body of parents or guardians. Therefore, if you are a parent of a child with this disorder, you must maintain adequate physical and emotional care for yourself, as it will help you obtain the energy you require.

Here are some tips for doing just that:

Schedule time for yourself. Including a proper diet, exercise, rest, and leisure activities in your routine is essential. You can use a calendar, planner, or organizer to make sure you set aside time for yourself.

Find out if a support group exists for parents of children with ADHD near you. If you didn't find any groups in your area, search online, or talk to your doctor about starting one or finding another related group that might help you.

CHAPTER 8: STAYING ORGANIZED

How to stay organized with ADHD

Getting and keeping organized is difficult for people with ADHD. Essential items become misplaced and difficult to find, chores are challenging to accomplish, and work appears overwhelming. ADHD symptoms are exacerbated when your life and environment are cluttered and disorganized. Adult ADHD symptoms such as hyperactivity, restlessness, concentration difficulties, and other symptoms make it challenging for people to concentrate on tedious chores like getting organized.

It's a vicious cycle: ADHD makes organization difficult, yet disarray exacerbates ADHD symptoms, making getting your life in order even more difficult. That does not imply that you must give up and live in misery and disarray. Take up the challenge, get your life on track, and things will flow better after that. The ADHD organization and time management strategies for adults listed below can help you stay afloat and swim ahead.

1. Create a system that works for you: Have a logical place for everything and put it back there after use. This will help you to perform effortlessly and smoothly, even under pressure. Use ADHD

organization charts, color coding, containers for storage, and other techniques.

2. One of the essential ADHD organization tools is lists. Keep track of tasks, deadlines, and other key dates by writing lists or using one of the many apps designed for the purpose.

3. Set your phone or computer to send reminders for appointments, events, and other important dates ahead of time.

4. Carry a notebook (or use your phone) with you at all times so you can work on your lists and jot down crucial thoughts. Having many notebooks stashed in various locations can be beneficial while some prefer a central location with one notebook.

5. Pin or write reminders to yourself on bulletin boards or whiteboards.

6. Choose a planning system that works for you and stick with it.

7. Use applications to help you stay organized if you have ADHD. There are numerous apps available to assist with organization and time management. Examine the numerous possibilities and choose an ADHD-friendly app to assist you. Look for one with the features and style you desire.

8. Hire an ADHD coach or a professional organizer. These experts come to your home or business to show you how to organize your life with ADHD.

How to Make Peace with Your Clutter

The workstations and residences of many adults with ADHD are untidy. If you thrive in those conditions, it's time to make peace with your well-ordered chaos. If not, learn how to avoid becoming overwhelmed by clutter. Adults with ADHD can benefit from these clutter-control tips:

1. Use baskets/containers without lids (e.g., boot box, gloves/hat/scarf box, kitchen spice box) for grouping similar things.

2. Make sure there is a wastebasket in each room.

3. In rooms where you read, put a magazine rack.

4. De-clutter for 15 minutes daily (throwing and putting things away, filing, if necessary).

5. Every room should have at least one junk drawer. Put items in that drawer if you aren't sure where they should go or if they don't have a place yet.

Handling Procrastination

Procrastination may be a constant battle for people with ADHD. Procrastination is made more likely by the primary symptoms of ADHD, such as inefficient time management, forgetfulness, and a lack of focus. People with ADHD may struggle to maintain their motivation to finish a task or get started. You may be procrastinating without even recognizing it. Procrastination can become a difficult habit to break after a while. This can result in a great deal of worry and other negative consequences, such as a loss of self-esteem.

1. Determine why you procrastinate.

The first step to getting a handle on your procrastination over certain activities is to figure out what's causing it. Take a look at any areas where you're having trouble. What emotions come to mind when you consider completing these tasks? What are the ideas that run through your head? It may be beneficial to jot down this information.

2. Break tasks down into manageable steps.

Extensive, challenging activities are frequently the ones that we delay. They can be overwhelming, especially if we don't know where to start. Mentally breaking down a task can be difficult for someone with ADHD, so writing out the steps might be beneficial. Determine ways to split up the assignment into manageable parts by working backward from the deadline. Make each step clear and actionable – something you can do and check off.

3. Make use of a timer.

Even when each step is put down, you may still feel overwhelmed while looking at your task list. You can use a physical timer or a smartphone app. Set a timer for 5 or 10 minutes and commit to working on the task until it is completed. Then, when the timer goes off, you can either continue the activity or take a 5-minute break. This aids you on multiple levels: it provides a more accurate sense of time passing, informs you of how long a task will take, and gets you started.

4. Make Your First Move

Getting started is usually the most challenging part. While you may still stop in the middle of your assignment, you will have completed a portion of it. Once you get started, you may discover that the process is not as challenging or painful as you anticipated. Find a solution to make the task even more accessible if it still seems too challenging. For example, instead of writing 500 words, start with 50. To stay going longer, try to capitalize on the momentum you've built up by getting started.

5. Reward yourself.

The reward system in ADHD brains is often dysfunctional, causing the brain to prioritize what it perceives as extremely stimulating or rewarding. However, things that are rewarding in the short term are usually harmful in the long run. If you're used to watching TV or playing video games as distractions from your job or obligations, see if there's a way to turn such activities into a reward for completing chores.

Dealing With Mind Clutter

Remember that we don't have to do it all at once. It's best to start small and manageable. We can also start with what really bothers us and immediately feel the benefit. Whatever your method, remember what your motivation is for eliminating clutter.

Remember your reason for doing the task. For instance, if you start a project to eliminate your clutter, make sure you make that decision because you need it and not because it's trendy. Removing clutter is something you *want* to do, not something you *should* do. If you feel happy and your creative clutter doesn't impact your life, continue. That's great!

167

Eliminating clutter does not always have to do with our possessions. We must also think about eliminating clutter from time commitments that are not aligned with our values, negative thoughts that weigh on our minds, and wasted time spent on social media.

Excessive clutter is often a symptom and cause of stress and can affect all areas of our lives – from the time it takes us to get things done to our finances to our mental health.

Tips for removing mind clutter

1. Be practical. Don't sign up for a class at 8 am if you don't like getting up early. Set yourself up for success by scheduling your classes during times of the day that you know you'll be most attentive and when you know you can make it on time. Many students with ADHD find it hard to get up in the morning. If this happens

to you, don't sign up for the early morning classes, even if they seem like "the best class ever!" It doesn't matter how good a class is if you're not there to participate.

2. Work first, play later. College campuses are full of temptations that can distract you from completing your work, and college students with ADHD often have to work very hard to do well. Schedule specific study periods in a quiet place, and stick to the plan. Reward yourself with fun social activities, but discipline yourself to work first and play later.

3. Be proactive. Get the necessary support before a crisis arises. All colleges have resources available to help students with ADHD succeed. Contact the Learning Support Services office before you arrive on campus, find out what documentation they need to confirm

your ADHD diagnosis, and ask what services they can offer you. If you find that you are struggling to pass a class throughout the semester, contact the learning support services office and your teachers as soon as possible to see what disability support they can give you. If the semester is almost over, there is very little they can do to help you, but if you do it earlier in the semester, there are plenty of options for help.

Tools to Help You Focus

1. Calendar and task planner

Aside from the apparent benefit of remembering appointments and commitments, using this application regularly will aid you in accomplishing two goals:

a. Visualize time passing, making it "real" – this is a strenuous effort for many persons with ADHD.

b. Overcome "big project overwhelm" by breaking more extensive activities into smaller ones and scheduling them over time.

Writing things down can also make you feel more accomplished because it lets you visually tick things off your list and see how far you've progressed.

2. Pill container on a keychain

Taking their medication on time can be difficult for anyone, but it can be practically impossible for someone with ADHD. While you can set a reminder and keep your meds in the same spot to maintain some consistency, you never know when life will throw you a curveball. Always have a supply of medication on hand in case of an emergency.

3. The command post

A logistical headquarters is required in every residence. Set up a location near the door for a: Whiteboard — to transmit critical messages, a family calendar, and a drop-off and pick-up point for your keys, papers, handbag, kids' backpacks, library books, incoming dry cleaning, and other items. Look for ideas on Pinterest that are appropriate for your situation.

4. Charging station number four

Here's a critical component to consider when it comes to command centers. Why spend 30 minutes every morning driving yourself and everyone else in the family insane looking for your phone or laptop just to be caught with a dead battery?

5. The Pomodoro Technique

The word "Pomodoro" means "tomato" in Italian, although you don't need a round red timer to use this method. Any timer will suffice. Setting a time restriction is one way to entice yourself from procrastination and into a task (e.g., 10 minutes toward clearing off your desk). Pick up a copy of the book and learn everything there is to know about this time-saving strategy that is ideal for anyone with ADHD.

CHAPTER 9: FOCUSING ON A NEW YOU!

"If you don't know exactly where you're going, how will you know when you get there?" - Steve Maraboli

Live Boldly – Free of Guilt and Shame

We hope as you're reading this book that you're picking up some valuable tools you can use to make the big and small changes that will affect the trajectory of your entire life. We want to empower you to live a full life you once thought impossible.

Living with attention deficit hyperactivity disorder might result in jumbled thoughts and difficulties concentrating. This lack of concentration can cause problems at school, at work, and at home. You may set lofty goals only to become distracted or abandon them entirely. While you may not be able to force yourself to concentrate, there are certain things you can do to help you stay focused.

Learning what works best for you is the first step in improving your attention. Not every method will work for your specific case. Finding the best ones for you could take some trial and error.

1. Strive for clarity.

How motivated you are to complete a task partly depends on how well you understand it. Vague projects and jobs can be intimidating. You may not know where to begin. Asking clarifying questions can help if you're unsure or distracted about what you're doing. The more information you have, the easier it will be to establish an action plan. Usually, with tasks like this, the hardest part is to just begin. Once you start, they become clearer.

2.   Break down tasks.

Some tasks are more challenging to complete than others. When faced with a huge undertaking, breaking it down into smaller goals may be beneficial. Small goals within a larger goal can help a project not feel like it's taking too long. Smaller goals might also help you feel driven by maintaining a sense of accomplishment.

3.   Maintain a tidy work environment.

Thoughts aren't the only source of distraction. Sitting in an untidy environment might provide its own set of distractions. In the middle of drafting an email, you might feel compelled to reorganize those files. Maybe you're fumbling with a stapler that's broken. Maintaining a clean and orderly workspace can help you avoid becoming sidetracked.

4. Make a strategy.

Breaking down and clarifying tasks go hand in hand with planning. You may have limited objectives and a good understanding of the intricacies, but if you don't know where to begin, you may never get started. Making a plan keeps you focused on your objectives and allows you to build a timeline to keep yourself on track.

5. Find a relaxation technique that works for you. Inattention isn't necessarily related to jobs or projects when you have ADHD. You can become distracted in

talks, or you might find yourself skimming extensive documents rather than reading them properly. Relaxation training may be the answer when you need a quick focus strategy. Deep breathing techniques or meditation can help you focus and reset your train of thought.

Goal Setting

This goal-setting technique can help ADHD adults stay motivated and have fun while working toward their objectives. What is the best way to set up your goal? Choosing which objective to work on can be one of the most challenging aspects of goal setting. We frequently have a long list and can't decide where to begin. Alternatively, we may strive to create highly ambitious, big-picture goals rather than more attainable chores. Here's a way to get around this. Go inward and assess your feelings instead of gazing outwards at paper stacks, unpaid bills, incomplete tasks, or frightening projects like painting a room or planting a large garden. Which items on your to-do list make you nervous? Which items will make your life miserable if not completed soon (think: would my electricity be switched off? I should probably pay that bill!)? You'll have a better notion of which aim to start with if you look inward and take your ADHD "temperature." It's the one that, once checked off your to-do list, will make you feel better.

Staying Motivated

If you live with ADHD, you might find it difficult to stay interested in certain tasks or activities, but there are ways to help you get things done.

Women's overall perceptions of ADHD, in terms of how they experience the consequences of the disorder, are closely related to how they conceptualize the disorder (e.g., as a gift or a curse), as well as the degree to which they feel able to control their symptoms. Some women describe ADHD either in positive or negative terms, for example, as a gift with positive aspects or a curse that is incompatible with a normal life.

Some women can also identify personal strengths and positive learning outcomes from the challenges they have faced. Several perceive their positive traits as partly related to their ADHD, such as high energy, creativity, determination, ability to get easily interested and excited about new things, adventurousness, and willingness to take risks.

Despite misconceptions, lack of motivation does not have anything to do with laziness. Attention spans can wander if your goals and tasks are dull and boring. Many goals can feel burdensome, whether it's arranging a vacation or scheduling job interviews. Here are some things to think about.

- Break your goal down into smaller, more manageable chunks.
- Make a list of the steps you'll need to do to reach your objective.
- Make sure your objectives are reasonable. For example, if you want to enhance your health in the following year – a big-picture objective — it may appear to be a difficult task. Consider other possibilities, like walking, if you can't afford a gym membership.

Know Your ADHD and Own Your ADHD

There are many aspects of keeping a house and raising children which are rewarding and creative. Look for positive experiences to share with your children. Women with ADHD who feel they are "driven crazy" by the frequent interruptions of their children, who need to take time alone to ease frayed nerves, who fear being labeled as "poor housewives" and "bad mothers" need to understand and accept themselves and their ADHD. They also need to be understood and accepted by their husbands, their families, and friends. These are women with ADHD struggling valiantly against demands which are difficult if not impossible to meet. They need to learn not to measure their success in terms of making beds and washing dishes, but to celebrate their gifts - their warmth, their creativity, their humor, their sensitivity, their spirit. And they need to look for people who can appreciate the best in them as well.

There are many stories about what it's like to live with attention deficit hyperactivity disorder (ADHD). Is it a good thing? Is it a calamity? Neither? Both? If we had advice for anyone living with ADHD, it would be to stand up and claim it. Take a moment to hold your head higher and work that diagnosis like a red-carpet celebrity. We might as well make the best of it since we feel like we're being examined anyway, right? It's not always simple to embrace every symptom of ADHD or ourselves, but we can always own our ADHD. We aren't outcasts. We aren't helpless, hopeless, or lost. We are also strong, capable, and creative individuals who are capable of accomplishing anything we set our minds to. Here's how to claim your ADHD and be confident in your skin.

1. It's okay to accept your diagnosis.

What's more, guess what? It's okay to love having ADHD, believe that it makes us unique, and appreciate how our minds work. No, we can't do things the way most of the world expects us to, which can make school and work challenging, but we shine when we can use our talents and ingenuity to solve issues, explore our passions, or help others.

2.   Have confidence in yourself.

When you have ADHD, it can be tough to be confident but establishing confidence in your abilities and the unique way you see the world is the most pleasing thing you can do to take control of your condition. Owning your ADHD and being proud of what you can do rather than concentrating on your flaws will give you the confidence you need to face the day.

3.   Remember that a sense of humor is beneficial.

It's not all fun and games for people with ADHD. The condition can be aggravating, exhausting, and humiliating, and we all know how tough it can be for those closest to us. No matter how lovable we think we are, we can be challenging to deal with. It's part of the journey to own every aspect of our ADHD, even the less desirable qualities. We are halfway there when we accept that we can be forgetful, bothersome, perplexing, worrying, reckless, and even angry.

4.   Let go of perfectionist thoughts.

Learning to own your ADHD requires letting go of preconceived beliefs and the notion that you must, or even could, be perfect. Own up to your peculiarities – they distinguish you. Own the differences that make you unique and the characteristics that set you apart from others. Take control of your brain's gorgeous swirling turmoil. To learn how to operate with it, you must first own it.

5.   Ignore the rules.

Okay, some ground rules must be followed. But who says you must act, think, or be a certain way? Living your most extraordinary life your way requires owning your ADHD. And taking control of your ADHD means doing what's best for you and your family in the way that makes the most sense to you and them. Nothing will be able to stop you from being the solid force you will be once you own your ADHD.

The Power of Self-Acceptance

Accept who you are, how you think, and what makes your ADHD brain sing to gain true power and productivity. In this section, learn how to maximize your abilities and develop the tactics you'll need to get things done. Understanding and dealing with how we think is critical to strategizing and taking effective action. Change is a process; the better we grasp it, the less complicated it is. Here are a few options for getting started.

1. ADD/ADHD honesty is the first step toward self-awareness.

Self-awareness begins with a list of your strengths and weaknesses:

- Who are you and who are you not?

187

- What are you likely to do or not?

- How do you operate versus how do you wish you worked?

You risk establishing a life or making choices that aren't right for you if you don't have self-awareness. You may build tactics to improve your strengths and compensate for your ADHD issues once you know who you are and how you perform (or don't). You can take action to reduce your frustration triggers if you're aware of them. When you know what gives you energy, you can set aside time in your calendar to do it.

2. Make self-acceptance a habit.

You may not like everything about yourself, but accepting who you are, how you think, and how you do things increases your chances of getting things done. Create a judgment-free zone in your mind and let go of your expectations of yourself. You are a one-of-a-kind blend of personality, history, ADD, LD, IQ, genetics, birth order, abilities, and environment. People who embrace themselves are happier and more productive, according to studies! We are less likely to *react* and more capable of *acting* when we accept ourselves. Break free from the self-critical guilt trap. Instead of helping us go forward, guilt traps us in a web of failure and regret.

CONCLUSION

The increasing research on females with ADHD is encouraging, yet it is still in its infancy. We are beginning to look at the impact of brain-based hormonal fluctuations and genetics, in addition to societal influences and expectations. The evidence shows that there is significantly greater impairment and a higher risk of negative outcomes for girls and women with ADHD. We owe it to these women to get the word out and to educate them and others on the facts.

This book provides a better understanding of females with ADHD to increase recognition and awareness. We have explored why women with ADHD keep falling through the cracks and provided insights on how you can unmask the bias, discover your strengths, and take charge of your life and relationships.

While both males and females are diagnosed with ADHD, females do not have access to adequate treatment due to gender biases in diagnosis. Sadly, because school teachers and parents tend to focus on males who can't sit quietly or speak out of turn, some girls will grow up without the same treatment. Because of the unique presentation of their symptoms, females with ADHD are often underdiagnosed. As a result, females are more likely to be overwhelmed, nervous, sad, and have low self-esteem due to their ADHD symptoms. In general, both males and females with ADHD have a high rate of co-morbidity with other mental health issues. Females with ADHD are more likely to have anxiety or depression, and while their ADHD may go unnoticed, their secondary diseases may be mistaken as central.

The appropriate intervention can have a positive impact on affected girls and women with ADHD, their families, and more broadly on society leading to increased productivity, decreased resource utilization, and most importantly, better outcomes for girls and women.

If you are a woman with ADHD, you should know that it is a very treatable condition. As overwhelmed as you may feel, know that you can feel better. There is a lot you can do to regain control of your life, instead of having ADHD control you. There is no one-size-fits-all way to handle the condition. Ultimately, the right treatment plan is the plan that works for you.

One more thing

If you enjoyed this book and found it helpful, I'd be very grateful if you'd post a short review on Amazon. Your support does make a difference, and I read all the reviews personally so I can get your feedback and make this book even better. I love hearing from my readers, and I'd really appreciate it if you leave your honest feedback.

Thank you for reading!

REFERENCES

1. Bachmann CJ, Wijlaars LP, Kalverdijk LJ, Burcu M, Glaeske G, Schuiling-Veninga CC, Hoffmann F, Aagaard L, Zito JM. Trends in ADHD medication use in children and adolescents in five western countries, 2005–2012. European Neuropsychopharmacology. 2017 May 1;27(5):484-93.

2. Chang Z, D'Onofrio BM, Quinn PD, Lichtenstein P, Larsson H. Medication for attention-deficit/hyperactivity disorder and risk for depression: a nationwide longitudinal cohort study. Biological psychiatry. 2016 Dec 15;80(12):916-22.

3. Jensen CM, Steinhausen HC. Comorbid mental disorders in children and adolescents with

attention-deficit/hyperactivity disorder in a large nationwide study. ADHD Attention Deficit and Hyperactivity Disorders. 2015 Mar;7(1):27-38.

4.   Briars L, Todd T. A review of pharmacological management of attention-deficit/hyperactivity disorder. The Journal of Pediatric Pharmacology and Therapeutics. 2016;21(3):192-206.

5.   Faraone SV, Asherson P, Banaschewski T, Biederman J, Buitelaar JK, Ramos-Quiroga JA, Rohde LA, Sonuga-Barke EJ, Tannock R, Franke B. Attention-deficit/hyperactivity disorder. Nature reviews Disease primers. 2015 Aug 6;1(1):1-23.

6.   Young JL, Goodman DW. Adult attention-deficit/hyperactivity disorder diagnosis, management, and treatment in the DSM-5 era. The primary care companion for CNS disorders. 2016 Nov 17;18(6):26599.

7. Jain R, Jain S, Montano CB. Addressing diagnosis and treatment gaps in adults with attention-deficit/hyperactivity disorder. The Primary Care Companion for CNS Disorders. 2017 Sep 7;19(5):24623.

8. Sayal K, Prasad V, Daley D, Ford T, Coghill D. ADHD in children and young people: prevalence, care pathways, and service provision. The Lancet Psychiatry. 2018 Feb 1;5(2):175-86.

9. Quinn PD, Chang Z, Hur K, Gibbons RD, Lahey BB, Rickert ME, Sjölander A, Lichtenstein P, Larsson H, D'Onofrio BM. ADHD medication and substance-related problems. American journal of psychiatry. 2017 Sep 1;174(9):877-85.

10. Adult attention-deficit/hyperactivity disorder (ADHD) [Internet]. Mayo Clinic. 2019 [cited 2022 Jun 1]. Available from: https://www.mayoclinic.org/diseases-

conditions/adult-adhd/symptoms-causes/syc-20350878

11.   Angel T. ADHD (attention deficit hyperactivity disorder): What is it? [Internet]. Healthline. 2021 [cited 2022 Jun 1]. Available from: https://www.healthline.com/health/adhd

12.   sm-lynne. Latest research shows growing out of ADHD is unlikely [Internet]. SafeMinds. 2021 [cited 2022 Jun 1]. Available from: https://safeminds.org/news/latest-research-shows-growing-out-of-adhd-is-unlikely/

13.   CDC. Data and statistics about ADHD [Internet]. Centers for Disease Control and Prevention. 2021 [cited 2022 Jun 1]. Available from: https://www.cdc.gov/ncbddd/adhd/data.html

14.   Sharon Saline PD. ADHD statistics: New ADD facts and research [Internet]. ADDitude. 2006 [cited 2022 Jun 1]. Available from:

https://www.additudemag.com/statistics-of-adhd/

15.   Polanczyk G, de Lima MS, Horta BL, Biederman J, Rohde LA. The worldwide prevalence of ADHD: a systematic review and metaregression analysis. Am J Psychiatry [Internet]. 2007;164(6):942–8. Available   from: http://dx.doi.org/10.1176/ajp.2007.164.6.942

16.   ADHD and More [Internet]. Blogspot.com. [cited 2022   Jun   1].   Available   from: https://adhdandmore.blogspot.com/2009/04/ad d-adhd-and-understanding-how-brain.html

17.   Robinson S. Understanding how the ADHD brain works [Internet]. Look! We're Learning! 2014 [cited   2022   Jun   1].   Available   from: https://www.lookwerelearning.com/how-the-adhd-brain-works/

18. Neurodiversity: Is ADHD a true mental disorder? - ADHD: Attention deficit hyperactivity disorder [Internet]. Gracepointwellness.org. [cited 2022 Jun 1]. Available from: https://www.gracepointwellness.org/3-adhd/article/13863-neurodiversity-is-adhd-a-true-mental-disorder

19. Drugs.com. [cited 2022 Jun 1]. Available from: https://www.drugs.com/mcd/adult-attention-deficit-hyperactivity-disorder-adhd Christiansen S. What Is ADHD? [Internet]. Verywell Health. 2020 [cited 2022 Jun 1]. Available from: https://www.verywellhealth.com/adhd-attention-deficit-hyperactivity-disorder-included-definition-symptoms-traits-causes-treatment-5084784

20. Bbrfoundation.org. [cited 2022 Jun 1]. Available from: https://www.bbrfoundation.org/ask-an-

expert/how-is-adhd-diagnosed Migration F. Attention-deficit/hyperactivity disorder (ADHD) in children [Internet]. NCH Healthcare System. 2001 [cited 2022 Jun 1]. Available from: https://nchmd.org/health-library/articles/con-20155299/

21.	Fried C. What Happens if ADHD is Left Untreated? [Internet]. Reekooz.com. 2021 [cited 2022 Jun 1]. Available from: https://www.reekooz.com/what-happens-if-adhd-is-left-untreated/ ADHD Myths & Misconceptions [Internet]. HealthyChildren.org. [cited 2022 Jun 1]. Available from: https://www.healthychildren.org/English/health-issues/conditions/adhd/Pages/Myths-and-Misconceptions.aspx]

22.	Jones H. How to recognize ADHD in women [Internet]. Verywell Health. 2021 [cited 2022 Jun

13]. Available from: https://www.verywellhealth.com/adhd-in-women-common-signs-and-symptoms-5211604 .

23. ADHD in women 101 [Internet]. Kaleidoscopesociety.com. [cited 2022 Jun 13]. Available from: https://www.kaleidoscopesociety.com/adhd-in-women-101/

24. Lmft SSM, Novotni M. Female ADHD test: Symptoms in women and girls [Internet]. ADDitude. 2017 [cited 2022 Jun 13]. Available from: https://www.additudemag.com/self-test-adhd-symptoms-women-girls/

25. Rausch SL. The daydreamer: Why ADHD in females is underdiagnosed [Internet]. ADHD Online. 2022 [cited 2022 Jun 13]. Available from:

https://adhdonline.com/the-daydreamer-why-adhd-in-females-is-underdiagnosed/

26. Wu B, PhD MD. Why ADHD diagnosis in women is still a challenge [Internet]. ADHD Online. 2022 [cited 2022 Jun 13]. Available from: https://adhdonline.com/why-adhd-diagnosis-in-women-is-still-a-challenge/

27. Sokol L. ADHD: Too often misdiagnosed in females [Internet]. Women's eNews. 2021 [cited 2022 Jun 13]. Available from: https://womensenews.org/2021/08/adhd-too-often-misdiagnosed-in-females/

28. Rucklidge JJ. Gender differences in attention-deficit/hyperactivity disorder. Psychiatr Clin North Am [Internet]. 2010;33(2):357–73. Available from: http://dx.doi.org/10.1016/j.psc.2010.01.006

29.   CDC. Treatment of ADHD [Internet]. Centers for Disease Control and Prevention. 2021 [cited 2022   Jun   13].   Available   from: https://www.cdc.gov/ncbddd/adhd/treatment.ht ml 9.   Medications used in the treatment of ADHD [Internet]. CHADD. 2018 [cited 2022 Jun 13].   Available   from: https://chadd.org/for-parents/medications-used-in-the-treatment-of-adhd/

30.   Cherney K. ADHD medications list [Internet]. Healthline. 2020 [cited 2022 Jun 13]. Available from:

https://www.healthline.com/health/adhd/medic ation-list

31.   ADHD   alternative   treatment   [Internet]. Understood.org. [cited 2022 Jun 13]. Available from:

https://www.understood.org/en/articles/adhd-alternative-treatment-what-you-need-to-know

32.	Katie Hurley L. ADHD and relationships [Internet]. Psycom.net - Mental Health Treatment Resource Since 1996. Psycom.net; 2017 [cited 2022 Jun 13]. Available from: https://www.psycom.net/adhd-and-relationships/

33.	How ADHD affects relationship with your partner? [Internet]. Mango Clinic. 2021 [cited 2022 Jun 13]. Available from: https://mangoclinic.com/how-adhd-affects-relationship-with-your-partner/

34.	Adult ADHD and relationships - HelpGuide.Org. [cited 2022 Jun 13]; Available from: https://www.helpguide.org/articles/add-adhd/adult-adhd-attention-deficit-disorder-and-relationships.htm

35. No title [Internet]. Mind-diagnostics.org. Mind Diagnostics; 2022 [cited 2022 Jun 13]. Available from: https://www.mind-diagnostics.org/blog/adhd/adhd-in-adults-and-relationships-how-to-navigate

36. The best ADHD management tools [Internet]. Healthline. 2017 [cited 2022 Jun 13]. Available from: https://www.healthline.com/health/favorite-healthy-adhd-management-finds

37. Boyd A. If you're diagnosed with ADHD, procrastination may be A struggle. Here's how to manage [Internet]. Betterhelp.com. BetterHelp; 2019 [cited 2022 Jun 13]. Available from: https://www.betterhelp.com/advice/adhd/if-youre-diagnosed-with-adhd-procrastination-may-be-a-struggle-heres-how-to-manage/

38. Peterson TJ. ADHD and how to stay organized [Internet]. Healthyplace.com. [cited 2022 Jun 13]. Available from: https://www.healthyplace.com/self-help/adhd/adhd-and-how-to-stay-organized

Printed in Great Britain
by Amazon